CRACKING THE MAN CODE

*Understanding Your
Husband's Heart*

Dr. Joe Pettigrew

Cracking The Man Code

ISBN 9798306337333

Published by *ITZ Publishing*

Unless otherwise noted, Scripture notations are from the New International Version (The Holy Bible) copyright 2011 by *Biblica*, an International Bible Society publishing ministry.

Printed in the United States of America

Cracking The Man Code will help you to understand just what men want in their marriage. You will discover that the Word of God has a great deal to say about both what women want and what men want.

Many books have been written to help men understand what women want. However, women are the ones that purchase and read most books that are sold-not men. Since men don't buy or read these books, it is understandable that they continue to do what they have always done and you continue to be frustrated. So many authors continue to write more and more books, believing that the previous books just didn't hit the mark with men. The solution just may be a book written for women instead of men. We continue to read that women want love and men want respect. So if that is true, what does that mean for you and what you can do to improve your marriage. I hope you enjoy what has been prepared for you. I hope it will change and improve your marriage.

Joe

Table Of Contents

CHAPTER 1

R.E.S.P.E.C.T

For many women, love is synonymous with emotional connection and care. But to many men, respect is love. Without it, they feel unappreciated, inadequate, and even rejected. God wired men to thrive in an environment where their competence, decisions, and efforts are affirmed. When this critical need for respect is unmet, they often grow discouraged or distant. It's not because they're prideful or demanding, but because respect is part of their God-given design.

These seven letters catapulted a preacher's daughter from intercity Detroit to the top of the Billboard charts, and decades later, when Aretha Franklin belts out her signature anthem, everyone knows exactly what she needs. RESPECT is a song written and originally released in Memphis, Tennessee, by Otis Redding; however, it didn't become a blockbuster hit until two years later when the famous Queen of Soul recorded it. Otis Redding wrote the song as a man's plea for respect and recognition from his woman. Both versions of this blockbuster hit were tremendous popular. While we know that both men and women desire to be respected, you may realize that you have discovered a secret regarding what your husband is thriving for. Respect for him is his most important need!

Bookstores are full of books about *what women want*. There was even a blockbuster movie starring Mel Gibson and Helen Hunt that focused on answering this intriguing question. Would it be good if your husband knew what you wanted and what you were thinking all the time? Think about that before you answer. This important concept hasn't just evolved from generation to generation; it is actually found in the Bible. You may be thinking that all sounds great, but what does it mean? *"However, each one of you also must love his wife as he loves himself, and the wife must respect her husband."* Ephesians 5:33

Your husband has heard many times how important it is for him to love you. He may have a different way of showing it than you desire, but he knows it is important. The same is also true for you; you know how important respect is to your husband, but the way you show him respect may be different than what he wants. With these two trains headed toward each other, there is a need for a discussion about what both men and women need in their marriage. With a clear view of what men desire, you can have a real concept of what your job is and how to go about it. Once you have a better idea of how to do this, many relational landmines will be avoided. The result can be more extraordinary. Couples often believe they are getting no closer to their goal of a great marriage than when they started their journey. Somedays you may wonder if you have learned anything about this very complicated human being called your husband. The disconnect is really pretty simple:

- Many books have been written to help men understand what women want, however, women are the ones that purchase and read these books-men don't.
- Since men don't buy or read books, it would be useful if they did but they don't.
- So authors continue to write more and more books, believing that the previous books just didn't hit the mark with men.
- The solution may be a book written just for women, by a man, about how women can show their husband respect.

You want your marriage to become stronger and more intimate. However, your sweet, loving, clueless husband continues to operate in the dark by trying harder to do what he has always done. Let's look at the other side of the coin—what do men need and how can you help them receive it. This is a subject that doesn't get a great deal of attention in our culture. When you find the answer to this question, your marriage will get better and better.

In her best-selling book, *Being the Strong Father Your Children Need,* Dr. Meg Meeker talks about how men are often disrespected in today's culture. If you were to form your opinion of the average husband today based entirely on the examples presented by the media or on television, you'd come to the conclusion that all husbands are idiots and losers. Your husband just may not be like those portrayed in current sit-coms. Seeing husbands like this, certainly makes for nightly humor as we think of men as bumbling, childlike, and self-centered creatures. This is, however, very unfair. Most husbands think with their brains, love their wife and want to be great fathers.

What is being streamed into your living room, for you and your children to watch, is an image of a man that I believe certainly exists, but is not the norm. Our society has gone through an extended period of demeaning women, so maybe it's now time for men to be stereotyped negatively by the media. However, when you spend time in front of your television, you will see how today's men are portrayed— and it's not positive. Take a look at shows like those listed here and you will notice what the media wants us to think of husbands and fathers:

Modern Family
The Family Guy
Life in Pieces
Two and a Half Men
Everybody Loves Raymond
Married with Children
King of Queens

In a recent article, Bishop Robert Barron of PBS fame, referred to this effort as the Homer Simpsonization of men. *Don't get me wrong: I'm a big fan of The Simpsons and laugh at Homer's antics as much as the next guy. But the father of the Simpson family is stupid, boorish, drunk most of the time, irresponsible, comically incompetent, and childish.*

You will notice this prototype in many of today's family sitcoms, where the female lead is fit and gorgeous and the male lead is a deadbeat Neanderthal. We have come a long way in portraying women as competent individuals at home and in the workplace. During the time women were demeaned, it seemed as though they fought hard to get their rightful place in society returned to them. We know the work is not finished in this area; however, it appears that the tide has now shifted—and shifted in a significant way. In a recent survey, two-thirds of men said they are proud of their efforts to support their family and become the husband their wife needs. Despite all their efforts to improve, your husband has to sit back and watch other men being endlessly lampooned by the media as not much more than a lazy sperm donor. Most families on television are shown with either a loser for a father - or with no father figure at all.

At a time when there is a desperate need for robust male role models in our country, your husband is undermined to such an extent he is often regarded as an amusing appendage of no actual use to his family. Men are portrayed as only interested in watching ballgames, drinking beer and being waited on around the house. They are showcased as lazy slobs only interested in sex, food, and being the King of the remote control.

Many men just don't fit this stereotype. They are trying to be involved in the activities around the house, and helping raise their children. So what does this matter? The question should be, what can you do to help your husband regain his place in society and especially at home.

Men have always been defined by their work. It is essential to a man's self-esteem to be seen as someone who is valuable and important in the eyes of the world and, most of all, someone who is essential in the eyes of their family. After many years of success as a senior executive, my friend was forced to resign from a position. He was the President's right hand, so when the President was relieved of his position, the Board decided to wipe the slate clean. The position carried with it prestige, power, respect, and, yes, financial stability. Never in his life had he been in this situation before, and in the blink of an eye, he was figuratively shown the door. His ego was destroyed. His status as the provider of his family was crushed, and for the first time in his life, he didn't know what to do. As the primary breadwinner for most of his marriage, he was unemployed, depressed, and embarrassed.

When he walked in the door of his home that afternoon, his wife immediately realized something was wrong. He didn't know where to start, as he wanted to be strong, in control, and save face. He saw it as his job to be the strong person in his marriage and he thrived on being respected at work and at home. His wife listened, asked the appropriate questions, and ensured that he knew whose side she was on. She told him they would be alright because she believed in him. She reinforced his position as the family leader, although he didn't feel much like the leader. Then, she knew what he needed, so she left him alone. That evening, they sat down, and she began to do what only a Godly wife can do—she began to build her husband back up. He was down, but she systematically started the process of restoring his pride and his ego. She knew the issues he had been dealing with at work and helped him put things into perspective. Much publicity came out in the small town regarding his removal. Friends that were once very close didn't return calls. People he had worked with closely didn't seem to remember his name. However, through it all, one person was his rock. His wife treated him as the family's leader and respected him by allowing him to have the same voice in decisions he had always experienced.

There are words that can boost a man and make him want to be better. These words can sometimes be magical in his quest to be respected, especially when they come from you. Words like:

I believe in you: This is an ego booster. These words will keep him going when he faces adversity in life.
I trust you will make a great decision. It is so important to men when you show confidence in them regarding making decisions.

You are strong. Your husband will probably act like this is unimportant; however, when men hear these words, it adds spring to their steps.

I feel safe around you. One of your husband's top priorities is to protect you and his family. If you acknowledge him in that area, he will try even harder.

I appreciate your efforts. Everybody loves to be recognized. The more he hears this, he will learn to return the compliment, but this support is critical.

You are great at what you do at work. Every man wants his wife and family to know and appreciate that he is good at what he does.

I don't want to be with anyone else but you. Your husband wants to know that he is the man, the one you love. These words will go a long way to reassure him of this.

Even though your husband knows he is married to someone extraordinary, it doesn't hurt when you surprise him. Several years ago, a man had some of his buddies over to watch a big game, and they would not stop commenting on how old and small his television was. They were relentless with their kidding regarding his need to join the new century by purchasing a new large flat-screen television. He told them he would talk to his wife about it, and they would decide what to do. Then the kidding really started, *Who's the boss in this house, you or your wife?*

He didn't realize that his wife was listening to all the friendly banter, but he knew she always had his back. Without his knowledge, she decided to show him precisely what respect was. After his friends had gone, she briefly discussed that it really might be time for them to look into getting a new television if he was going to have his friends over to watch ballgames together. She told him to think about it and she would do whatever he decided.

Because of her support, he now wanted her help in selecting one. They weren't looking for just any television, but a super large screen with all the bells and whistles. It may be years before we would buy another television, so purchasing the most up-to-date technology was essential. He was proud of his due diligence because he had researched his purchase online. He even reviewed Consumer Reports to ensure he wouldn't make a mistake.

They drove to the shopping center to look for their prize. He discussed the sophisticated analysis he had gone through with the salesperson. He wanted to impress his wife and the salesperson with his knowledge. Out of the corner of his eye, he noticed she was wandering around, looking at all the televisions that were on display. When salespeople see this behavior, it is like a hungry wild animal discovering a wounded animal—they were ready to pounce. The sales staff began asking her questions, however, to his delight, she insisted they speak with her husband as he was the expert on the subject. She was very complimentary of the one he had chosen, and she proudly said in front of the store personnel,

Honey, you get whichever one you believe to be the best. I trust your judgment.

She had built him up to be the world's smartest husband. When he got into the car, he told her how much he appreciated what she had done, and she acted clueless. What do you think happened after later that day? She had taught him a valuable lesson about respect, and she received a valuable lesson back about how a husband can love his wife. She was treated like a queen after that.

You and your husband may have grown up in a time when his role models were firmly opinionated men. Whether this was the best example for him or not, it may be the reason he acts the way he does. If you think about it, in the past most school leaders have been men, and most teachers were women. It was also true that coaches, sports referees, pastors, judges, law enforcement officials, doctors, and politicians were almost always men. Because men were in these roles, it had nothing to do with whether or not they were the smartest or more capable for those positions; it was just the culture of the times.

Today we find an increasing numbers of husbands who are simply checking out. One-sixth of men between the ages of 25 and 34 are unemployed and have stopped looking for work. Women are outpacing men in both college attendance and graduation. Suicide rates for middle-aged men continue to rise. Fathers are now absent from more than one-third of

American homes. Women are leading Boy Scout troops, coaching ball teams and are many times the primary bread winners. There are many factors behind these statistics, however, our society continually feeds men the message that they are unimportant and their families don't expect much from them. An outspoken actress and controversial talk show host recently said that women had almost made it. *We have figured out how to replace men in every aspect of life but one —sperm donors. We will one day find a way to remove them of that responsibility as well.*

The Apostle Paul believes it is important for women to respect their husband. Notice what he doesn't say. He doesn't say, respect your husband the way you see on television. He doesn't say, respect your husband like your friends respect their husbands. He doesn't even say, respect your husband like your mother respected your father.

Respect for men has diminished over the years. It is certainly true that some men don't deserve respect because of how they have treated their wives and children. Many women are in the workforce today working diligently to provide essentials for their families because their husbands have disappeared and deserted them. While men desire to be respected, many have walked away from their responsibilities and chose to leave their families behind. God has specific roles for the husband and the wife, and when we spend time in His Word, we have a higher chance of a successful marriage and a quality family life.

I hope you are married to a great man. I hope that he loves Jesus and takes his role seriously as the spiritual leader of your family. I hope that your home is filled with God's love. If he demonstrates these qualities, then thank God for your husband. If your husband is not the Godly man you desire, pray for God to take over your husband's heart. He is waiting to be asked and He is in the business of changing hearts.

Men deeply desire to please their wives, but they sometimes get confused on how to do that. Your contentment and happiness means the world to them and if you are unhappy about your life, it affects him deeply. Your husband may even begin to wonder if he is the reason for you being unhappy. When you are happy and he can hear it in your voice, it makes him feel good as your husband. If a wife doesn't believe in her husband or is continually dissatisfied, he will feel hopeless and unloved. If he doesn't get the affirmation, support, and encouragement he needs at home, then unfortunately, men often seek respect elsewhere.

Men need a helper, a partner, a coach, a confidant, and an encourager. It's true that sometimes men are not the most natural creatures to love or to communicate with. Nothing is more glaring than the need and desire of a man to be respected, and the primary person who can do that— is you. Men need respect from their wife, not because of their pride, but because secretly, many feel inadequate. Males have very fragile egos although they don't want to admit that. Even the most competent and self-assured man will buckle under the idea that his wife doesn't believe in him.

God calls you to respect your husband—not because they deserve it every moment, but because it reflects the love and reverence you have for God. When you show respect, you're weaving God's design into your marriage, creating a union that blesses not only you and your husband but also the kingdom of God.

Your challenge is simple. Tell your husband one thing you respect about him everyday—something meaningful, specific, and totally unexpected. Watch how it uplifts him... and maybe makes him rethink how he treats you.

CHAPTER 2

GOD HAS A PURPOSE FOR YOUR MARRIAGE

What an extraordinary, messy, beautiful bond marriage can be. God's design for marriage is both profound and practical, wrapped in a covenant of love and faith that mirrors His own relationship with us. Yet, let's be honest, there are days when we reflect on that big question, *Why did we get married?* And sometimes, the answer feels like it's hiding between the laundry pile and the tenth disagreement about paying the bills. You must rediscover the reasons behind your *Yes* and lean into the divine purpose of your union. Please laugh a little, learn a lot, and hopefully emerge with a renewed heart full of gratitude, grace, and joy for the person you vowed to love as long *as we both shall live.*

Why did you get married? For sex, romance, companionship, security or children? All these are great reasons, and becoming one with another human being can also be terrific. God has woven into the DNA of the human heart a craving for oneness. A pastor friend once said, *weddings are easy; marriages are difficult.* The couple desires to plan a wedding; God intends to design a marriage. The couple wants to focus on where the bridesmaids will stand; God wants to embed a feeling of forgiveness. A wedding can happen in twenty minutes with little effort, but a marriage takes year after year of alert, wide-eyed attention. Marriage is what you create after the wedding is over.

Do you remember the words you agreed to on that particular day when you got married? Chances are, you do. You were nervous, afraid, and excited. So much preparation had gone into the big day that you were just glad it was finally happening. Many words were spoken that day. The pastor had words of wisdom for you out of the Bible. Your parents had words of wisdom for you based on their years of experience. Your friends, even those that weren't married, had words of advice for you. You heard words that day that will stick in your mind forever. Words like:

> *To have and to hold from this day forward*
> *For better, worse, prosperous, and poorer*
> *In sickness and health*
> *To love and to cherish, till death do us part*

When you got married, you loved him, but you hadn't thought about richer and poorer, better or worse, sickness and health, or till death do us part. You just knew you were in love; you wanted to live with him, and it seemed like it was time to take the next step in your relationship. Marriage is the ultimate partnership. You go from being your own person to sharing a life—your space, your time, and, yes, possibly even your bank pin number. Marriage is messy, beautiful, trying, rewarding, and if we're honest, sometimes it's just downright confusing. But, above all, marriage has a purpose.

That's right—God has a purpose for your marriage, and it's far greater than perfectly coordinated home decor or who gets to choose what's for dinner. Marriage is a covenant, a reflection of God's design for love and partnership. And while it's easy to get caught up in the daily grind—those tense conversations about whose turn it is to fold the laundry or who emptied the dishwasher last—there's a divine call buried beneath the routines.

Marriage is your daily invitation to encourage, nurture, and support someone else. Maybe your husband had a rough day at work, and he needs to hear, *I believe in you.* Maybe it's patiently helping him with a decision he's been struggling with for weeks. When you support each other, you build a foundation of trust and unity. And here's one of the rewards— your marriage becomes a safe space for you both to chase after God's purpose for your lives, together.

We have all heard the phrase, w*e're better together.* When it comes to marriage, it's absolutely true—but unity doesn't mean uniformity. God put two different people together because they're stronger as a team. Genesis 2:24 says, *"That is why a man leaves his father and mother and is united to his wife, and they become one flesh."* Unity in marriage means aligning your hearts, values, and purposes—not necessarily agreeing on whether pineapples belong on pizza. The world is watching you and your husband. Your children, your friends, even that random couple at dinner sitting behind you are watching you. A unified, God-centered marriage becomes a testimony of His grace, hope, and power.

Marriage is hard work; no one's denying that, but it's also a treasure chest of joy and laughter. Proverbs 5:18 encourages us to "*rejoice in the wife of your youth*," a reminder to cherish the person you've committed to—even as you both evolve and grow. Marriage isn't the perfect Hallmark movie; it's about faithfully wading through the trenches together, finding joy in the mundane, and laughing at each other.

Ultimately, God's purpose for your marriage is so much bigger than you and your husband. It's a reflection of His glory, a tool for sanctification, and a way for both of you to live out His plan. God doesn't expect you to do it all on your own; He's with you, guiding and sustaining you as you grow together. If you've felt like your marriage is running on fumes, take heart—God's not done with you yet. He's got plans to prosper you as a couple and give you hope and a future. So ask God to lead your marriage into deeper unity, purpose, and joy.

Marriage is beautiful, challenging, chaotic, and rewarding— all wrapped up in one covenantal union. If you've been married for more than five minutes, you know it's not always smooth sailing. There's toothpaste squeezed from the middle, mismatched socks left on the floor, and laundry pilled up everywhere. But at its core, marriage is so much more than two people sharing a cellphone plan or arguing over whose turn it is to go to the grocery. But what exactly is God's purpose for your marriage? Out of the billions of possible arrangements, why did God create this sacred bond between you and your husband? And how, amidst the trials and joys, can understanding His purpose strengthen your marriage?

Your marriage is not just about you and your husband. Turns out, your union serves a much bigger plan. Marriage reflects the love, commitment, and selflessness demonstrated in God's relationship with us. Think about it. God's relationship with His people is rooted in covenant—a sacred promise. Marriage mirrors that covenant. When you said *I do*, you weren't just committing to put up with each other's quirks. You were entering into a covenant that reflects God's ongoing, unbreakable love for His people. Every sacrifice you make for your husband, every moment you choose grace over irritation, shows a glimpse of God's love in action. It's a reminder that love isn't about convenience. Love is about choosing each other—even on the messy days when patience feels far away.

Sometimes we like to romanticize marriage. You know—the *you complete me* kind of thinking. But marriage wasn't designed to complete us because that's God's job. Instead, marriage is one of the tools He uses to refine us. Marriage has a way of making us painfully aware of our imperfections. Marriage will show you that patience, is a work in progress. God hones our ability to love selflessly. It's not about keeping score or waiting for your husband to deserve kindness. Instead, it's about growing in humility, learning how to serve, and becoming the best version of yourself—not for your sake, but for God's glory.

Marriage is supposed to be a safe haven—a refuge from the storms of life, a place where grace abounds. Our world can be pretty harsh. Work stresses, societal pressures, unkind feedback about your new haircut—it's tough out there! Marriage offers a sanctuary, a place to come home to, and an assurance that you're loved, regardless of life's challenges. Your husband will say things he shouldn't say and he will forget special occasions. But the beauty of it all lies in offering grace and forgiveness.

How many times have you had this thought about your husband: *If they would just change (insert habit here), life would be so much better?* But here's the twist—marriage isn't about fixing your spouse to fit your preferences. Marriage encourages both of you to grow. God didn't gift you a partner so you would have someone to fix. He gave you a partner to challenge, support, and for you to grow alongside. Whether it's encouraging patience, building a stronger faith, or working through conflict together, marriage creates space for growth.

When we think of mission fields, we usually imagine far-off places filled with unfamiliar languages and cultures. However, your marriage is a mission field. How you treat each other is a witness to the world. Through your partnership, you model God's love, faithfulness, and humility.

Don't underestimate the ripple effect of a strong, Christ-centered marriage. By showing how love can thrive within God's framework, you inspire other couples to seek Him in their relationships too. Your marriage isn't just about the two of you—it's a light that shines outward, impacting more people than you can imagine.

Your marriage is not just a contract—it's a covenant. It's not about perfection—it's about grace. To those of you currently in the trenches of day-to-day married life, here's your reminder to pause, breathe, and look at the beautiful work God is doing in your marriage. It's not without challenges, but it's also filled with opportunities for grace, growth, and joy. The next time you argue over something that doesn't matter, remember this—you're representing God's kingdom, one discussion at a time.

God manifests His plan for flourishing relationships in marriage—a union of two uniquely gifted people bringing their whole selves, quirks and all, to the table. Through marriage, you discover that your husband isn't just your friend or confidant; he's also your teacher and the lessons are humbling sometimes. What's amazing about God's design is that it's as much about individual growth as it is about togetherness. A healthy marriage challenges you to be a better version of yourself, to pour yourself into love so completely that it spills back into every relationship around you—family, friends, coworkers, even strangers.

Marriage is a lot like embarking on a two-person expedition. You need a shared vision and complementary strengths to chart unknown territories. God's plan is designed to combine your individual callings into something extraordinary together.

At the heart of it, God's plan for marriage is more than just coexistence. It's a partnership forged in love, built on trust, and maintained through a steadfast faith that both of you are stronger together than apart. The goal isn't perfection; it's progress.

We must not be fooled by Hollywood's happily ever after endings—marriage isn't a final destination; it's continuing education. Every argument, misunderstanding, or bad day offers two roads: an opportunity for growth or the temptation to dig in and hold grudges. Real love is patient, forgiving, and learns on the job.

Marriage has a way of revealing our rough edges. What if instead of resisting this, you embraced marriage as a tool God uses to help shape you into a better version of yourself? If there's one truth about marriage, it's this: *It's a daily commitment*. Marriage, like faith, isn't a one-time decision. It's your small, daily acts of choosing each other that build a bond so strong, even life's toughest storms can't break it.

In God's design, marriage isn't a job—it's an adventure. Yet here's the thing—marriage is God's idea. And like everything

God creates, it's not just good, it's really, really good. But, if you're like most married couples, you might be wondering at times: *What does God actually want out of this thing we call marriage? Why did He design it in the first place?* His plan for marriage isn't as mysterious or unattainable as we make it out to be. Although, it's probably more challenging and countercultural than we'd like it to be.

Marriage, at its core, is a reflection—a holy reflection—of God's relationship with His people. Look no further than Ephesians 5, where Paul takes us all on a spiritual crash course in God's plans for husbands and wives. It's here we're given marriage's ta-da moment. *"For this reason a man will leave his father and mother and be united to his wife, and the two will become one flesh...This is a profound mystery—but I am talking about Christ and the Church"* (Ephesians 5:31-32).

Marriage is supposed to be an earthly representation of the gospel. That through your relationship with your husband, people can understand something about God's relentless, sacrificial, never-giving-up love? God's blueprint for marriage is big. It's designed to point people—your kids, your friends, those nosy neighbors next door—toward Him. It's not just a partnership for tackling your to-do list or a convenient tax-filing status. It's a sacred relationship crafted to reflect the love, grace, and unity that exists between God and His people.

God's love for His people is constant, forgiving, and selfless. And—ready for it—you're called to love your husband that way too. Ephesians 5 doesn't mince words when Paul tells husbands to love their wives *"just as Christ loved the church and gave himself up for her"* (verse 25). And what about you? It means respecting your husband, even when your first reaction is to remind him of what he is doing wrong. What we love about God's plan for marriage is that He doesn't expect you to show that kind of love from your own strength. Because you can't. There will be days when your wedding vows feel less like a promise and more like a suggestion.

The same love Christ pours into you daily is the love you pour out into your marriage. We're talking about that fruits of the Spirit things—gentleness, kindness, patience, and OH YES...self-control. It's His power, not yours, that transforms your *I can't deal with my spouse right now* moments into grace-filled opportunities to reflect who He is.
God's plan for marriage is not about your agenda, comfort, or five-year ambitions. Why? Because marriage, at its best, is about serving one another. Jesus *"made himself nothing by taking the very nature of a servant"*. That's called *agape* love —the selfless, self-sacrificial, *I'm-putting you above m*e kind of love.

God didn't create marriage to make you happy. He created it to make you holy. And in that holiness, you'll discover something far better than fleeting happiness—you'll find joy. God's ultimate plan for marriage is rooted in His desire for unity, sacrifice, and deep intimacy. It's a picture of what it means to love, serve, and forgive like Jesus. And even on difficult days, when it feels like you're speaking different languages, you can lean into the promise that God is in your corner, equipping and perfecting your marriage.

Have you forgotten God's purpose for your marriage? Have you allowed the world to steal the joy of being married from you? Has society replaced it with PTA meetings, bake sales, children's activities, the iPhone, or TV? Do you need to be reminded that you were brought together with your husband for a purpose? You were brought together to spread the gospel of Jesus Christ to a world that is sometimes too busy to find Him. Friends and neighbors will look at your marriage and see something different. They see a man and woman connecting around something more substantial than themselves. They will see open forgiveness expressed to each other. They will see respect and love alive and well in your relationship. They will see children exposed to Jesus and have His teaching at the center of their lives. They will see something different in your marriage and may want you to tell them what it is.

CHAPTER 3

MEN WERE MADE TO PROTECT AND PROVIDE

Marriage is designed by God Himself. And within this sacred bond, men were given a unique role to protect and provide. If you're already smiling nervously, wondering where this conversation is headed, don't worry. Before you dismiss this chapter as another heavy-handed take on biblical manhood, take a breath. Protection and provision—when rightly understood—aren't about stereotypes or societal pressures. They're deeply rooted in God's design for men to lead with humility, serve with grace, and love sacrificially. It's not about demanding respect; it's about earning trust.

Your role in this conversation matters tremendously. While this chapter emphasizes the unique calling of men to protect and provide, it thrives best as a team effort—a dance between two equally valuable partners in a marriage. The very foundation of marriage begins in Genesis, and it's in the early chapters that we see God placing Adam in the garden with two significant tasks: *"to work it and take care of it"* (Genesis 2:15). From the start, Adam was given a role to cultivate, nurture, and guard what God had entrusted to him.

When we talk about men being called to protect, it's more than wielding a sword (or, in modern terms, defending the family during awkward family reunions). Protection extends far beyond physical security. True protection is spiritual, emotional, mental, and yes, financial. Provision, too, goes far beyond a paycheck. While being a provider often includes meeting material needs, it's equally about providing emotional stability, spiritual leadership, and cultivating an environment where love and respect can flourish.

God has assigned roles for both husband and wife to fulfill—not to create division, but so that each can thrive in the purpose He's designed for them. For Christian wives, understanding the God-given role of your husband can bring clarity, harmony, and joy into your marriage. One of the most profound aspects of a man's biblical role is to provide and protect. Now, before we get into this, I know that phrase alone may have sparked a ping-pong game of thoughts in your mind. Perhaps it stirred up discomfort, or maybe it brought a sense of appreciation. Either way, we're going to unpack what this really means—not in the *1950s caricature of a husband* way, but in a way that aligns with Scripture, love, and God's design for marriage.

The Bible gives us a blueprint for marriage in the earliest chapters of Genesis. When God created Adam, He placed him in the garden, gave him work to do, and instructed him to care for creation. Adam was tasked with being a steward, cultivating the land, and ensuring it thrived. This is the origin of man's role as a provider. Later, we see Adam protecting what he was given. God created Eve as Adam's helpmate, someone who perfectly complemented him. When Eve was presented to Adam, he immediately recognized her as part of himself—his equal under God. While Adam may not have done the best job of protecting Eve from the serpent, his responsibility to care for, love, and shield her remained.

Fast forward to today, and that divine design hasn't changed. Society might try to rewrite the narrative, but God's blueprint still stands. Men were created to provide (not just financially) and to protect (not just physically). Marriage has its joys, but it also comes with its challenges. You didn't enter this covenant lightly, and just like any other aspect of life, it takes patience, prayer, and a deep reliance on God to navigate the complexities of wedded bliss. Now, picture this. It's been a long day—one of those endless days where the laundry somehow doubled itself, the kids have lost their minds, and what was once a clean kitchen is now a crime scene. Just when you think you can't take another minute of it, your husband comes home. He steps through the door, surveys the scene (taking in your frazzled expression), and instead of retreating to his *man cave*, he rolls up his sleeves and joins the fray. Dinner? Covered. Kids? Managed. You? Supported and loved.

From the very beginning, God designed men with a specific role in mind. Genesis 2 sets the stage. Before Eve enters the story, God gives Adam meaningful work to do—tending the garden, naming the animals, providing stewardship to God's creation. This was Adam's place as a provider. Then, when God sees that it isn't good for Adam to be alone, He creates Eve to walk alongside him as a partner. Later, in Ephesians 5,

Paul describes marriage as a reflection of Christ and the Church. He says, *"Husbands, love your wives, just as Christ loved the church and gave Himself up for her."* That love isn't passive; it's sacrificial, tender, protective, and all-encompassing. Men aren't just meant to go out and bring home a paycheck. Providing and protecting go much deeper —they embody a spiritual calling.

Your husband's God-given role involves more than financial provision or keeping intruders at bay. At its heart, he's called to provide spiritual leadership, emotional security, and Christ-centered guidance for your home.

The truth is, society often challenges these traditional roles. Is your husband striving to provide, even amidst financial hardship or job transitions? Acknowledge his effort rather than measure success solely by external standards like his paycheck. Maybe he's not leading with sermon-worthy prayers—but does he show faith in small, day-to-day ways? Does he prioritize attending church, keeping values Christ-centered, or offering quiet consistency? Take note of tangible ways he's guiding you and your family spiritually. Protection isn't just physical. When your husband speaks wisdom into a family crisis, defends your reputation, or looks out for your emotional well-being, he's fulfilling his protective role in wonderfully nuanced ways.

Now, what if your husband struggles to step into his role? This book wouldn't be complete without addressing the elephant in the room. Perhaps he's struggling in leading the family spiritually or he has faced failures that hinder his confidence as a provider. This is where grace and faith come in. Trust that while your prayers may feel unanswered today, God is actively working within your husband to bring about His plans. And don't forget community. Leaning on fellow believers can offer guidance during seasons when progress feels slow.

Your role as a wife is equally significant! Just like the Proverbs 31 woman, you are your husband's greatest champion. You embody strength and dignity when you create a space where he feels equipped to take on his role. Marriage isn't about keeping score—it's about teamwork. When you both surrender to God's design, you create a partnership that glorifies Him.

The role of provider and protector isn't a badge your husband earns; it's a calling he grows into daily with God's grace. Your role is to walk alongside him, offering prayer, encouragement, and the quiet assurance that you're in this together. Whenever the path feels unclear, remember this truth from Ecclesiastes 4:12: "*Though one may be overpowered, two can defend themselves. A cord of three strands is not easily broken.*"

Take heart! No marriage is without its hiccups, but every hiccup is an opportunity to lean in and grow closer as husband and wife under God's guidance. You've got this—

and more importantly, God's got you both. Protecting doesn't mean your husband needs to sleep with one eye open next to a baseball bat under the bed. Protection is multi-layered, and it's all about creating an environment where you and your family can thrive. There's something undeniably comforting about having a husband who walks you to your car in a poorly lit parking lot or checks that the doors are locked before bed. It's part of the way God wired men—to stand as protectors against external threats. Protection isn't just about shielding you from external dangers; it's about safeguarding your heart. A godly husband is intentional about protecting his wife from things like disrespect, emotional neglect, and even the daily stressors of life. If he knows you're overwhelmed, he steps in —not just with solutions but with support.

One of the most beautiful ways a husband protects his wife is by being her spiritual covering. This isn't about control; it's about being a prayer warrior for you and your family. Understanding your husband's God-given role as a provider and protector isn't about setting unrealistic expectations or holding him to a perfect standard of masculinity. It's about appreciating the unique ways God has designed him to lead, love, and care for your family.

Support Him: Be his biggest encourager. Celebrate his wins, even the small ones. Whether he fixes a leaky faucet or remembers to grab your favorite coffee creamer on the way home, take a moment to appreciate him.

There will be days when you butt heads, miscommunicate, or feel like you're carrying more than your fair share. But when you both commit to walking in the roles God has assigned, you'll find a beautiful rhythm—one where your husband's provision and protection bless your home and your encouragement and support inspire him to be all that God has called him to be.

Your role in this is no small thing. Sometimes, the weight men feel as protectors and providers aren't immediately visible. Words of affirmation go a long way. A simple *I appreciate everything you do for us*, can fuel your husband's heart more than you know. Respect and trust his efforts, even when they don't look perfect.

When my oldest daughter was going on her first date, it was the most stressful day of my life. My wife called to let me know she was excited and was getting ready for her big night. What big night? No one told me there was a big night. What are you talking about? My wife calmly reminded me that our daughter's date would arrive in about two hours. I had forgotten. I thought about calling my hunting buddies and having them show up at my house with a display of force. However, with no time to waste, I jumped in my car, and in record time, I arrived at my house about ten minutes before her date was to arrive.

I heard his car pulling into our cove, so I peeked out the window to get my first look at *Mr. Special*. I could hardly believe my eyes. He was driving a truck and it was covered in mud. As he was getting out I noticed that mud was also caked on his shoes. I told my wife that this was not going to be pretty because the young man didn't anything care about his appearance. She insisted that I keep quiet and be nice. I went downstairs and greeted the young man at the front door. Immediately, I noticed he had taken off his shoes outside on the porch, no doubt trying to trick me and keep me from realizing how unkempt he was. He was a very handsome and polite young man, but we fathers can see through things that mothers don't see. I invited him into the den, and we sat in chairs facing each other. I wanted him to sweat a bit, so we sat silently. Finally, we began some small talk, and my wife entered the room to break the tension. She asked if I would start a fire in the fireplace, and I told her I would be happy to; however, I didn't know where a lighter was. The young man spoke up and said that he had some matches in the glove compartment of his truck. I knew it. He was a dope smoker. He had his own matches.

I explained to my wife where he had gone when she returned to the room. When he returned and handed my wife the matches, I decided now would be an excellent time for me to be the protector of my house. To ensure the young man knew I was on to him, I discreetly inquired why he had matches in his truck. He told me they were a present from a lady in his church when he became an Eagle Scout—Strike One for me. I then asked why he took his shoes off at the door and why his truck was muddy. He laughed and told us that his father was a pastor of a small country church and on his way to our house, he saw one of the ladies from his church with a flat tire. He stopped to help her change it, and when he was changing the tire, his truck, which he had cleaned all day, got mud all over it. At the same time, while helping with the tire, he got mud all over his shoes, so he left them outside—StrikeTwo for me.

I admit I was just trying to be the protector and instead I came off looking like the resident idiot. When my daughter came down the stairs, and she looked beautiful. She asked me if I had met her friend. Her mother assured her we had met and that we had a *fascinating conversation*. The final blow to my ego was when my daughter asked her date if he had told me about the news he received earlier that day. I indicated that he had not. What else could he say that would make me feel worse? She proudly announced that he had been awarded the Presidential Scholarship earlier that day at school to attend one of the most prestigious Christian universities in America. Great—Strike Three. I congratulated him, and as they were leaving, I asked him what he would major in at college. He said that he was considering being a pastor. Of course, he was. Is there a Strike Four? All I wanted to do was protect my family.

Your husband feels tremendous pressure to protect you and your family. He will never feel good about himself until he feels his family is protected physically, mentally, and spiritually. When God gives one of His daughters to a man,

He expects the man to care for and protect her. Women are a gift from God to men.

God has blessed and honored your husband by providing him with a loving wife. And as his partner, you have a role in helping him be the provider and protector that he feels called to be. Your husband was created to defend what God has entrusted him, but he can't do it alone. He needs your help and God's guidance.

Women are very capable of protecting themselves, and there are many instances in which they do just that. However, God made men and women different; thus, due to the physical nature and strength God gave men, He has charged them with protecting their families. A man's physical nature and power are to be managed with grace and gentleness.

With all the changes that are going on in America, men are struggling to determine exactly what their purpose is. To live a happy, fulfilling, and productive life, he needs to know his primary purpose, his true mission regarding you and his family. While men and women often share these attributes, men generally gravitate toward being providers and protectors, and women gravitate toward being nurturers, and comforters. Your husband will experience the absolute joy of giving and using all the beautiful gifts and talents God has given him to succeed.

At a time in history, women were identified by questions like, *Are you married?* or, d*o you have a family?* While that is undoubtedly true in some instances, today women wear so many hats, the question is often, *How do you find time to get everything done?* However, the most common questions asked of your husband have remained pretty much the same, *What do you do?* or *Where do you work?* Men define themselves by what they do. When your husband's work is going great, things at home are usually great; however, the opposite is also true.

Something about getting married and having a family changes a man's perspective. Instead of dreaming of being a professional athlete, he aims for a good job where he can spend time with his family. Instead of a multi-platinum record deal he once coveted, he pursues health insurance, living in the right school district, or having a home in a safe neighborhood. Instead of wanting to be a famous astronaut, he dreams of raising one. This is maturity for a man. This is growing up for a man.

One of the saddest pictures is when a man fails to pursue providing for his family because he is stuck chasing the clouds of his youth. When men work to provide for their families, they serve the Lord. Whether a business person, a mechanic, a salesman, a lawyer, a teacher, a waiter, or working on a landscaper crew, all is in direct service to Christ. There is honor and goodness in work. God's love is seen each time a man brings home a paycheck. A man coming home to play with his kids after an exhausting day of work has shown us what Christ-likeness is.

CHAPTER 4

FRIENDSHIPS ARE ESSENTIAL

Many couples spend more time catching up on emails than seeing their neighbors, coworkers, and old friends. You may often joke about spending another weekend becoming *a boring old married couple.* Yet friends can support—not detract from—your marriage. Maintaining older mutual friendships can also strengthen the bond between you and your husband. Having people around who see the two of you as a unit, admire your relationship, and expect you to stay together can sustain you through times of doubt or distance. While a close friendship with your husband is vital for a stable relationship, close friendships outside of the marriage are also meaningful. One of the biggest killers of passion in marriage is the meaningless time you and your husband spend together. This monotonous coexistence is what often comes to define many marriages.

Your marriage remains your priority outside of your relationship with Jesus Christ. But without friends, your relationship with your husband and God can suffer. Some women expect their husband to meet all their social and emotional needs. The phrase implies that, since married people have each other, they no longer need friends. This exaggerates the risks young couples already face: setting unhealthy expectations and looking at each other as the sole source of total fulfillment.

Do you agree there are things a close friend can say to you that no one else can say? The Bible states that your marriage and your friends are essential to you. Many are married to a husband who is a great friend, and they love being together. Just consider that your relationship with your husband can be much stronger than any best friend relationship.
Your best friend probably knows you hate sushi, and being around smoke makes you sick. Your husband can quote your social security number, what medication makes you swell up, and the story behind the tattered and disintegrating quilt that you still proudly display in your bedroom. Your husband can anticipate how you'll react to any given situation. He knows what you love more deeply than anything. He knows your fears, experiences, and failures that cut you to the core. Your husband knows what you don't want to talk about and realizes what you just can't put into words.

How many friends do you have? Five? Twenty? Hundred? How many of them are close friends that you can trust with anything? How many of them consistently encourage you and build you up? While gaining many friends on social media is easy, we all need more than just passing acquaintances who fill our newsfeeds with funny dog pictures or pictures of adorable babies.

If there's one thing that most married couples can agree on, it's that marriage doesn't come with a manual. Sure, there's scripture, great advice from relatives, maybe a book or two on how to make marriage work, but once you're in it, marriage becomes a start-to-finish, *figure it out as you go* type of adventure. Nowhere in this great adventure are there instructions on how to balance marriage and friendships as a woman of faith. And yet, friendships—particularly for women—are an absolutely vital part of a strong, joyful, God-centered life. Yes, you need your girlfriends. Outside of marriage. Outside of family.

I know what some of you might be thinking. *But my spouse is my best friend! Why do I need other friends?* It's a beautiful sentiment, and you should absolutely strive for deep friendship with your husband. But, being a best friend doesn't mean being the only friend—and here's where your faith, scripture, and a bit of shared wisdom come into the conversation. Marriage is a blessing, yes. But friendship? Oh, what a gift. God, in all His goodness, didn't just give us His Spirit to guide us—He gave us each other. And whether it's knowing inside jokes, praying over that thing they can't talk about out loud, or simply sitting in silence, the presence of a godly girlfriend is a reminder of His glory.

Married women need girlfriends, no matter how full their lives are. You are never too busy, too far, or too worn out to make space for the kind of friendships that change everything. If you're married and balancing faith, family, and everything else life throws at you please take this to heart. You need girlfriends. Yes, girlfriends. Real ones. The kind who knows the ugly-cry face you make when you laugh too hard or how you need exactly 30 minutes of venting before you can move on from whatever stress the day threw at you.

Some of us equate marriage with the idea that our husband will and should meet all of our emotional, spiritual, social, and intellectual needs. The truth is, as amazing as your husband might be, one guy can't carry the weight of being everything for you. That's not biblical—it's just unrealistic. God gave us community for a reason. And for women, that community includes having close, faith-filled girlfriends who can walk life's wild terrain with you. Now, don't get me wrong—you are not being encouraged to overlook your marriage. Marriage is sacred, a beautiful gift designed by God to reflect His love for the Church. But marriage is not meant to be lived in isolation from others.

Once you get married, friendship feels harder. Life is busy, and if you have young children, it can feel next to impossible. Between signing permission slips, working through meal plans, and attending church bake sales, where's the time for this mystical girlfriend bonding we are talking about? Here's where we need to be reminded of something critical: friendship isn't a luxury; it's a necessity. And in marriage, it's not just you who benefits—your husband and your family experience the ripple effects of what happens when you make space for friendship. Why? Because your girlfriends encourage you to be the best version of yourself. They remind you that you're not just *Mom*, *Honey*, or *That Lady Who Organizes All the Church Bake Sales*. You're still you—the woman fearfully and wonderfully made by God. Your friends help you remember that truth on hard days when you might doubt it. They pour into you so that you can pour back into others from a cup that isn't bone-dry.

Girlfriends who are anchored in Christ don't just listen when you're venting about how your husband made a mess again, nor do they silently nod as you panic over whether other perfect moms at school are judging your store-bought brownies. Instead, they add something deeper—they point you back to God through all your joys, struggles, and questions. That's the kind of spiritual encouragement we all need.

Have you felt guilty about spending time away from your husband and kids to be with friends? There's this sneaky little narrative that tells us good wives or mothers don't need their own time. But God didn't make you to live solely in service to others. Remember how Jesus Himself often stepped away from the crowds, even from His disciples, to pray, to rest, or to connect with God? If the Son of God needed to carve out time from His busy ministry for specific, intentional renewal, don't you think loving yourself enough to spend time with friends might fit somewhere in the plan?

Cultivating friendships takes intention, not perfection. It's okay to start small. Call up another mom from the soccer team. Message a woman from church who seemed like she got your crazy comment during Bible study. Or, if you're an introvert, start with something as simple as sending a funny meme to someone you want to reconnect with.

Marriage is a beautiful calling but it's also exhausting. There's joy, sanctification, and, yes, the occasional overdrawn emotional bank account. Having girlfriends by your side isn't a distraction from your marriage—it's a gift to your marriage. Your husband needs to grab the kids one Saturday morning, make pancakes, and tell you to go meet your girlfriends. Because you know what? That coffee date may just refill a piece of the woman he fell in love with—and that's a blessing for the whole family. God made you for connection. So go ahead and call your girlfriend, plan that brunch, or send that text that reignites the bond. You need your girlfriends, and guess what? They need you, too.

Ultimately, friendships outside of marriage aren't just about women finding their joy. They're about honoring God by living fully into the relationships He calls us to pursue. Proverbs 17:17 tells us, "*A friend loves at all times, and a brother is born for adversity.*" These relationships are part of God's design for how we thrive as individuals and, by extension, as couples.

When you nurture friendships that encourage your faith, you're honoring your marriage by prioritizing your personal joy and spiritual renewal. Friendships are not competition. They're reinforcements. And when both partners in a marriage understand this, they unlock an even deeper level of unity and trust. Life can get busy, and it's easy to push friendships to the back burner. But don't forget—they're worth it.Husbands and wives often enjoy doing things completely different. There are things you enjoy discussing that he doesn't care to discuss. You enjoy antique shopping; he enjoys going to Bass Pro Shop. You spend time differently, and you even laugh at different things. What your children do may be hilarious to your husband and humiliating to you. However, having someone who enjoys many of the same things you want can make you happy and take the pressure off your marriage. Your husband really loves you; however, he is not capable of being what you need in every area of your life, and you can't fill that void for him either. There should be a close friendship between you and your husband; however, having him as your one and only best friend just might be hurtful or even a disaster for your marriage.

When you first met your husband, you were both living fulfilling and satisfying lives. He had his priorities and passions, and you had yours. One reason your husband was attractive to you was his life apart from you. The lives you lived before you met were essential to what made you want to marry each other. Your husband was not looking for a best friend or buddy but a loving, supportive wife. As you began spending more time together and getting to know each other, you likely had less time to engage in what you were doing before you met. Friends became expendable. The things you both did slipped down the list of essential things, and you wanted to spend every waking moment together. Some couples go so far as to entirely give up everything they previously found fulfilling and vital to spend all their free time together. The issue is, as you became fused, you became more and more dependent on each other to meet each other's emotional needs. This burdens both of you tremendously as your spouse feels responsible for filling the void for everything given up. This burden will create neediness, dependency, and sometimes resentment.

My friend once took his wife hunting. The key word is once. He love her very much, but hunting was something he had done for a long time, and he enjoyed doing it his way. Climbing up a tree with his tree stand took ten minutes, and he was ready. On this trip, he had to locate a two-man stand, which is always much more challenging. Once they got situated and prepared to hunt, his loving wife needed to go to the bathroom. There are few in the middle of the woods, and this problem is quickly solved for a guy. After taking care of necessities, his wife was now ready to share her most intimate thoughts and life issues since there were no distractions.He was looking for some quiet to hear the birds, the rustling leaves, and the many sounds he enjoyed. He hunted many days when he didn't shoot anything, but he didn't care as he just wanted to enjoy the experience.

When he failed to talk and sat quietly, she began to assume that he was upset and wished he had not brought her on the trip. Therefore, more questions are asked. She asked, *What are you thinking about?* He answered, *nothing.* She couldn't believe he was thinking about nothing, so she became more frustrated because he was shutting her out. He loved his wife. They go to ballgames together, church together, kids activities together, trips together, but they don't go hunting together.

One significant misconception is that if a couple has close friends, their marriage must not be trustworthy. While that is up to you to decide, that is normally not true. There are specific reasons why you both need to have close, Godly friendships. Scripture is filled with numerous examples of why friends are so important. You will find below some reasons why you should cultivate and hold onto such a special gift from God and why you should also encourage your husband to do the same:

For Encouragement. We all need someone that we count on to help us. Someone who knows you well also knows when to leave you alone and when to call. Whether you are having a great or an awful day, your friends are always there to encourage you. They want to celebrate with you when you have fantastic news and sit quietly with you when the dark clouds circle above. They help you to remember that God has everything under control, even if it doesn't seem like it now.

Ask Difficult Questions. When you are struggling and a friend asks how you are doing, it can be tempting to say, *Fine*. Godly friends, however, don't let you get away with this. They ask difficult questions to find out what is going on to determine how they can help you and, most importantly, how they can pray for you. Whether you are struggling with depression, a cheating husband, or struggling to stay faithful, your closest Godly friends want to know what's going on so they can be there for you. They sometimes ask questions you don't want to answer or have not considered.

Offer Godly Counsel. Advice is straightforward these days. Every time you turn around, you find many opinions, many directly opposing the others. Godly friends give you the guidance you can trust. Their information is based on Scripture and delivered with your unique circumstances and personality in mind. They won't just tell you what you want to hear. They'll help you figure out what God wants you to do in your situation.

Keep You Accountable: Being a Godly woman isn't easy, and you will mess up sometimes. Thankfully, Godly friends keep us accountable. They ask the tough questions to see what you are struggling with, and then they follow up consistently to know how you are doing. They don't do this to judge or belittle you but because they genuinely care about you and help you be a fantastic, Godly woman.

Pray for You. Whether you are sick, unsure about a decision, or just received big news, Godly friends are the perfect people to pray for you, and they are always happy to do it. They won't just say, "I'll pray for you," and then forget. They will pray with you, then go home and pray some more.

Loves Sacrificially. Jesus is the most exceptional example of a true Christian friend. His love for us is sacrificial, never selfish. He demonstrated it through his healing miracles and, more thoroughly, through the humble service of washing the disciples' feet and, ultimately, when he laid down his life on the cross. If we choose our friends based only on what they have to offer, we'll rarely discover the blessings of a genuine godly friendship.

Accepts Unconditionally. We discover the best friendships with others who know and accept our weaknesses and imperfections. We'll have difficulty making friends if we're easily offended or hold on to bitterness. No one is perfect. We all make mistakes now and then. If we look truthfully at ourselves, we'll admit we bear some blame when things go wrong in a friendship. A good friend is quick to ask forgiveness and ready to be forgiving.

Trusts Completely. A true Christian friend is trustworthy. We should only expect to share complete trust with a few loyal friends. Trusting too quickly can ruin, so be careful about putting your confidence in a mere companion. Over time, our true Christian friends will prove their trustworthiness by sticking closer than a brother or sister.

Keeps Healthy Boundaries. If you feel smothered in a friendship, something is wrong. Likewise, if you feel used or abused, something is amiss. Recognizing what's best for someone and giving that person space are signs of a healthy relationship. We should never let a friend come between our spouse and us. A true Christian friend will wisely avoid intruding and recognize your need to maintain other relationships.

One of the best things you can do for your husband is to remove the tremendous responsibility off his shoulders and cultivate some great girlfriend friendships. Your husband desires to be everything you need in life. However, with all his pressures, it comforts him to know that you have women with whom you can share your most profound concerns. Someone genuinely interested in the new wallpaper you are selecting for the kitchen or whether the picture over the fireplace is hung too high. Women who care about you. And extremely important, he wants to know that your friends want you to have a healthy marriage with him.

Marrying your best friend is enough of a cultural expectation that if you admit you didn't marry your best friend, some people would feel sorry for you. But here's the secret: you're the lucky one. You have a husband who isn't your best friend. And you have a best friend that you are not married to. They play different roles in your life, and you need them both. For Christians, marriage is a relationship set apart, wherein we assume the cares and concerns of our spouse in a way that supersedes any other friendship. You didn't marry your best friend. Instead, you married your husband, with your best friend beside you, to celebrate. It was the happiest day of your life. You got—and still have—it all.

CHAPTER 5

COMMUNICATIONS

Marriage, they say, is a gift from God—but sometimes, it feels like that gift should come with an instruction manual. One day you're united by vows of love that seem to echo through eternity, and the next, you're arguing over the correct way to load the washer and dryer. Thankfully for all of us, God has a lot to say about communication, and His wisdom can make all the difference.

When communication flows in a marriage, it's a beautiful thing—two hearts entwined, beating as one. You finish each other's sentences, you feel understood and cherished, and your talks can feel like a glimpse of God's perfect harmony. But when communication breaks down? It's like a runaway mine-cart, and suddenly, you're dodging accusations, frustration, and blank stares that scream, *are we even speaking the same language?*

But here's the good news—God doesn't just leave us to figure this all out alone. His Word is full of wisdom on how to relate to one another as husband and wife. Ephesians 4:29 encourages us to use our words to *"build others up according to their needs,"* and Proverbs 15:1 reminds us that *"a gentle answer turns away wrath."* Communication within marriage isn't just about talking more—it's about talking well, with love, patience, and a whole lot of grace.

One of the biggest misconceptions about communication is that it's simply about words. Maybe you're great at expressing yourself—spilling detailed explanations and heartfelt emotions. But here's the question: Is your spouse listening? And more importantly, are you listening? 1 Corinthians 13 describes love as patient, kind, not easily angered, and keeping no record of wrongs. Nowhere does it say love yells because someone misplaced the remote. When you communicate with your spouse, ask yourself:

Are you patient in your tone?
Are you kind in your words, even when you are upset?
Are you seeking unity or just trying to win the argument?

Marriage is sometimes correlated to a beautifully symphony. Many distinct instruments, with unique melodies, blended together to create a harmonious masterpiece. Well, that's the goal anyway. But every once in a while—or, honestly, way more often than we would like to admit—it sounds less like Bach and more like toddlers playing with pots and pans. And the culprit behind the noise? Communication. Or, more specifically, miscommunication.

Before we get too deep into the serious stuff, can we just take a moment to appreciate how funny marriage can be? Think about the last big misunderstanding you had with your husband. Was it about where to eat dinner? Maybe about how putting the toilet paper roll on the holder actually isn't optional? Life's funniest moments are often rooted in moments of misunderstanding because they reveal just how human we are.

During an argument a man looked his wife dead in the eye and said the infamous words, *You dropped the ball*. The ball, in this case, was forgetting to pick up the laundry that afternoon. Being the good and devout Christian woman she was, she spent the next week passive-aggressively labeling every ball she could find around the house with Post-it notes reading "NOT Dropped." It wasn't her finest hour, nor was it the most Christ-like response. Here's the thing about marriage—those little frustrations can balloon into monumental misunderstandings if we don't figure out how to talk to each other honestly and openly. And most importantly, with grace.

The gap between what someone says and what we interpret can be a cavern. You maybe the one jumping to conclusions and filling the gap with your own assumptions. Proverbs 18:2 reminds us, "*A fool takes no pleasure in understanding, but only in expressing his opinion.*" Ever found yourself too busy preparing your response while your husband is talking to actually listen? God's Word calls us to a higher standard of communication. James 1:19 gives clear advice on this when he says, "*Everyone should be quick to listen, slow to speak, and slow to become angry.*" True communication in marriage doesn't start with speaking; it starts with listening. It becomes less about whose fault it is that the cleaning didn't make it into the car and more about celebrating two imperfect people doing their best to love one another. None of this matters if we try to handle communication on our own. Without God, communication is just two flawed humans trying to make sense of one another. With God, there's grace and there's understanding.

When was the last time you prayed before having a difficult conversation with your husband? It's amazing how inviting Jesus into the conversation changes everything. Start by praying for clarity, patience, and wisdom. If you're really struggling, pray for supernatural kindness, because sometimes kindness in marriage requires nothing short of a miracle. Colossians 4:6 offers a beautiful framework for communication in marriage when it says, "*Let your conversation be always full of grace, seasoned with salt, so that you may know how to answer everyone.*"

It is helpful that you identify specifics to focus your attention on:

Clarify Expectations. Be specific about what you need or feel. It's not fair to expect your husband to read your mind.

Practice Active Listening. Repeat back what you hear to ensure you understand. For example, *What I'm hearing you say is that you're frustrated about the cleaning, not because I forgot it, but because it makes you feel like I wasn't thinking about you when I went to the store.* Perspective changes everything.

Use "I" Statements. Instead of saying, *You're always on your phone*, try, *I feel disconnected when we don't spend time together without distractions.* Small shifts make a big difference.

Be Generous with Apologies. Pride gets in the way of true reconciliation. Even if you only messed up 10% of the situation, take responsibility for your 10%.

Schedule Check-Ins. Regularly set aside time to talk—about feelings, about dreams, about everything. Make it fun! Have a cup of coffee or go for a walk together.

Laugh! Seriously, don't underestimate the power of humor. Next time you argue, try to find something lighthearted about it.

Ultimately, God didn't bring you and your husband together to live emotionally distant. Communication isn't just a practical tool; it's an act of love. It's how we honor one another, stay on the same team, and live out the covenant we entered before God. There will still be fumbles and misunderstandings—some mundane, some major—but His presence in our marriage smooths the edges. And through every conversation He is teaching us how to love one another the way He loves us—selflessly, abundantly, and without condition.

If there's one thing God continually teaches us in our marriage— it's to not take ourselves too seriously. Yes, marriage is sacred, but that doesn't mean it can't also be lighthearted and fun. A good laugh can break down walls that a perfectly worded argument might not.

My wife and I recently went to an estate sale in the oldest Texas town. Although I would rather have a colonoscopy, followed by a root canal, than go to this type of event, I went and smiled because I knew how much she enjoyed doing this. The house was a beautiful old Victorian mansion packed with junk ("antiques"). People were searching to find that unique treasure they couldn't live without. We went from room to room for about an hour, and I can confidently say, I didn't find anything I needed or wanted. The owner began sharing stories of her fifty years in the home. I was highly intrigued until she got to the point that she mentioned it was the first funeral home in the small town. She went on to tell us that the room we were standing in, used to be the embalming room. That was the end of my tour and my brief shopping experience so I picked up my pace and left as soon as possible. It didn't matter what bargains the funeral home had available, I was done shopping..

While outside on the porch, I saw my wife looking at a unique antique parlor pump organ. Many people were also looking at it, so it must have been quite a treasure. Being the mind reader that I am, I discreetly walked over to the owner and asked the history of the organ. I could tell it was valuable;

more than anything, because of how well I know my wife, I knew she wanted it. When my wife was not looking, I made the deal. I was brilliant, sweet, caring, and attuned to my wife's inner feelings.

A few hours later, my son-in-law picked up the organ. I reminded him how valuable it was old and ensured he realized how careful he needed to be with this irreplaceable antique. They showed up with the organ, unloaded it, placed it into its proper location, and we were ready for the unveiling. I called my wife into the living room to show her our new treasure. Her response was priceless! *What is this ugly thing doing in my house? That's not the organ from the funeral home is it? Why did you buy that hideous thing? Why did you buy this ugly albatross without asking me?*

Once again, I was reminded of how little I knew about the woman I had been married to for more than forty years. I tried to explain how the purchase happened and make sure she realized I was trying to please her. Her next statement was also priceless: After I saw this, *I was walking around and I actually wondered, what crazy person would purchase such a large ugly piece of furniture?*

Before your marriage, the primary focus of your relationship was on the many things you both had in common. But as time passes and your life changes, you often begin to see how different you and your husband are. This is especially true regarding the differences in how you communicate. Much has been written about women and men being from different planets and having their own cultures; the reality is that we have all grown up on the same earth, but we interact with each other in very different ways. It is interesting to study the communication differences between men and women; however, we must be careful not to stereotype and assume that all men and women will act a certain way.

Marriage communication also requires a sense of humor! There's a reason marriage vows include— for better or worse. God knew we'd need to laugh—not at one another but with one another—to survive the absurdities of being two flawed humans trying to build a life together. Take, for example, the age-old debate over your household thermostat. Many arguments have been waged between those with a spiritual gift for blanket hoarding and those with the unyielding belief that their body temperature is the thermostat's sole purpose for existence. And yet, amidst the ice-cold drafts and thermostat wars, what if this tiny battle became a running joke instead of an endless dispute? What if laughter replaced frustration in those repetitive disagreements that all married couples face?

Humor doesn't erase challenges, but it smooths the jagged edges and helps us keep perspective. God, after all, has a sense of humor—and He delights in our laughter and in marriages filled with joy. Marriage communication without grace is like baking without sugar. It's technically possible, but miserable for everyone involved.

Common Pitfalls and Godly Solutions:

The Assumption Trap. Imagine this scenario: Your husband sighs heavily for the third time, and before you know it, you're thinking, *What did I do now?* Spoiler alert—possibly nothing. Assumptions are the enemy of healthy communication. They thrive on partial truths and jump to conclusions God never intended you to leap toward. Instead of assuming, try asking. A simple, *Hey, what's on your mind?* can disarm brewing tensions and open a channel for genuine connection.

The Scorekeeping Spiral. 1 Corinthians 13, reminds us that love *"keeps no record of wrongs."* No list scribbled onto the tablets of your heart. No tally marks etched onto your memory of past grievances. Love doesn't keep score; it aligns itself with the grace we've received from Christ.

The Silent Stand-Off. While there's wisdom in pausing to choose your words wisely, silence weaponized as punishment is another story altogether. Healthy communication thrives on dialogue, and avoiding an issue doesn't resolve it—at best, it delays healing; at worst, it adds more tension. Instead, pray for words. Take to God what you're reluctant to take to your spouse first. You'll be surprised how prayer softens your spirit.

Marriage communication boils down to this—reflecting Christ in the way we love, listen, and extend grace to our spouse. It's less about winning arguments and more about winning at love, humility, and understanding. And here's the real beauty of it all—when you communicate with your husband in a spirit of grace and love, you mirror the relationship between Christ and His Church, a picture the world needs to see. There will still be missteps and days when it feels harder than it should, but marriage itself is a picture of God's work in you—constant, refining, and always worth it. With God at the center of your marriage, even communication challenges become opportunities for growth and greater connection.

Regarding communication within marriage, the following is a safe place to start and end. An experienced older pastor provided me with this morsel of knowledge, *In marriage, you can be right, or you can be happy. And I choose happy every time.* Being right often matters at the office and in other areas of your life, but being right is not rewarded in the bonds of marriage. It simply has no value. Sometimes, you must choose, *Do you want to be right, or do you want to be happily married?* Remember, being right in your marriage will get you nothing. Don't go for right; go for love. So how do you improve the communications between you and your husband? Consider a few ideas that may change your marriage quickly, permanently, and for the better.

Positive Attention. When you begin your conversation with positive affirmations, compliments, and affirmative statements, it sets you husband up to want to talk so that you can have a healthy discussion starting at the beginning. When you start with criticism, accusations, or pointed questions, he often locks up before you start.

Praise, Not Criticism. Certain types of positive behavior are more desired by your husband than others. He is indeed not a fan of criticism or comparison. However, finding ways to get the point across while he doesn't see it as critical is the success factor. Does the word "nagging" ring a bell?

Body Language. Communication is more about body language than words. Positive body language lets your husband know you are interested, not bored, not angry, and are very engaged in listening to what he is talking about. Crossed arms, glares, a blank stare, rolling eyes, lack of eye contact, and turning your back—-not so much.

A Christian marriage starts in the heart with the simple, fundamental truths that you were taught as a child: Be kind, have a tender heart towards people, and forgive others. Sometimes, it's hard to be kind to someone who doesn't show you the love you desire. It's often difficult to have a tender heart toward a husband who is just not lovable. And to forgive your husband when he has been a jerk—well, that's almost impossible.Why not ask your Heavenly Father to help you be more sensitive to how you respond to your husband when he is not very loving? Often, we have excuses that we use to justify why communication in our marriage is not as it should be:

I am just in a bad mood.

You told me you wanted to be left alone

I need time to be away from you and have some space

I just am frustrated, and it has nothing to do with you

I didn't hear you. Were you talking to me

I am tired of arguing with you

I was not ignoring you; it's all in your mind

Your husband should know when the laundry needs to be done and that your sweater can only be washed on a delicate cycle. It should be evident to him that you need his help when the kids' science fair project is a priority one night before it's due. And if you have to tell him you like the Antique Pearl paint for the shelves better than putrid Eggshell White, he doesn't even know you. The power of communication is especially essential in the bonds of marriage. And, by our words, we can destroy the very gift and purpose God has given us in marriage.

You and your husband may want to say a few things to each other every day.

Thank you.

I'm proud of you.

Good morning and good night.

We're in this together, to the end.

You're amazing.

I'm here for you, no matter what.

Have fun!
I love you.

We live in a cold, cruel world. Hearing that you're loved, smart, attractive, and fun from someone whose opinion you value can mean everything.

CHAPTER 6

YOU ARE HIS COACH AND CHEERLEADER

Have you ever thought that your husband might need a coach and cheerleader. This idea isn't about pompoms and pep talks—it's about fulfilling a God-given role in your marriage with a joyful and supportive spirit. Before you roll your eyes, let's break this down, coaching and cheerleading aren't about perfection. It's not about being his permanent motivational speaker or his personal life consultant, although it probably feels like you are wearing twelve hats already. No, it's about being the partner God designed you to be. One part mentor, one part encourager, and a whole lot of love in between.

Think about a coach. What do they do? They strategize, motivate, and point out areas for growth. They do so with wisdom, timing, and a whole lot of care. When you think about coaching your husband, it's not about telling him what to do. It's certainly not about telling him everything he's doing wrong, although this is often tempting! It's about gently guiding, humbly leading by example, and keeping Christ at the center of your relationship.

For example, if your husband struggles with prayer or being the spiritual leader in your home, what can a coach do? A good coach doesn't march onto the field screaming, dragging the players by their jerseys. They'd prepare the team to practice, set small attainable goals, and encourage progress. Maybe that means initiating prayer gently, like saying, *Hey honey, can we pray together about this week?* Or suggesting a devotional you can quietly read side by side without forcing the issue. Coaches work with the team, not above them. Coaching also requires patience. You know firsthand how easy it is to want instant change. But just like great teams aren't built in one practice, great relationships don't thrive from perfection overnight. Coaching takes prayer, grace, and steady commitment.

Cheerleaders don't just cheer when their team wins; they show up even when the scoreboard says zero. They hold up those intimidating signs that say, *We Believe in You*! or *You've Got this!* And maybe, just maybe, they do the occasional cartwheel when they feel the momentum build. The point is, even at the low points, they remain optimistic and ready to encourage. Sometimes it's hard to cheer when you feel like your husband forgot the emotional anniversary celebration of your fourth date or when he loads the dishwasher all wrong again. But here's the thing—cheerleading isn't conditional cheering. It's rooted in love, in the till death do us part vows you made before God. Your words of kindness and encouragement aren't just nice—they're powerful. Proverbs reminds us, "*A gentle tongue is a tree of life*" (Proverbs 15:4). When was the last time you cheered him on during everyday moments? A small thank you or I appreciated how you helped with the kids tonight can mean the world. And often, it may require biting your tongue. Cheerleaders do not throw insults when someone makes the big mistake. Instead, they clap, and they say, *You'll get 'em next time!* Loving your husband means choosing encouragement over criticism, faith over frustration.

Have you ever thought of yourself as a coach? Well, have you ever thought of yourself as a cheerleader? Now, you can be a cheerleader without the cute little outfits and large hair bows, and no, you don't even have to learn to tumble and flip. You can also be a coach without wearing bulky headsets, carrying a clipboard, whistling, and screaming. It is often said that a poor coach storms into the locker room at halftime and screams and humiliates his players for all the mistakes made in the first half of the game. However, this leaves the team with no time to fix any of the issues that caused their poor performance. A great coach realizes what didn't work in the first half and spends halftime building up his players and making changes so they will perform better in the second half.

Let's pretend it's halftime in your marriage, and you must decide if you are going to be a coach or a cheerleader. The secret is that you actually must perform both, to help your husband succeed. Your husband needs someone to build him up, and he also needs someone to help him improve in his walk with Christ and be the spiritual leader of the family. Marriage is unlike anything else in life—it's part joy, part challenge, part mystery, and sometimes, part *who left the toothpaste cap off again*? It's two flawed human beings committing to love and honor each other, no matter what life throws their way.

Whether or not you've got a pom-pom in hand, God has called you to be your husband's loudest cheerleader, his greatest encourager, and the coach who's there to guide and uplift him when he's down. But before you start worrying about how often you need to shout, *You've got this, babe!* from the sidelines, stick with me. We're about to unpack this incredible role—and have some laughs along the way.

Think back to any great coach or cheerleader you've seen. From high school sports to blockbuster movies, these are the people who inspire, motivate, and remind their team of what they're capable of. The truth is, there's nothing halfway about being a coach or a cheerleader. You're not in the stands, passively watching—no, you're up, engaged, fully invested, win or lose. And that's exactly the kind of active investment God asks of us within our marriages. Proverbs 31 paints a picture of a strong, faithful woman who works hard and encourages others. Verse 26 says, *"She opens her mouth with wisdom, and the teaching of kindness is on her tongue."* That's a description of a wife who uses her words and actions to motivate the people around her—especially her husband.

Now, you might be asking, *How do I practically coach my husband without feeling like a bossy know-it-all?* That's fair, and it's a balance! Coaching is not about criticism or control —it's about vision. It's about seeing the gifts, strengths, and talents God has given your husband and helping him to walk in that.

Okay, so maybe coaching comes naturally to you. But what about cheerleading? Maybe you're not the *Woo-hoo!* type, and that's okay. Being a cheerleader doesn't mean you have to yell enthusiastically every time your husband walks through the door. It's about bringing joy and positivity into his life in a way that lifts him up, even in the mundane moments.

Marriage isn't a solo event, it's teamwork at its finest. Ecclesiastes 4:9-10 drives this point home by saying, *"Two are better than one because they have a good return for their labor. If either of them falls down, one can help the other up."* Can you imagine if the coach abandoned the team mid-game or the cheerleader packed up her pompoms after one bad play? Marriage is the same way. God didn't design us to quit on each other; He designed us to persevere together. Your role is vital. Not because your husband can't succeed on his own, but because your encouragement, your gentle guidance, lifts him higher than he could go alone. Marriage is about pushing each other toward Christ with love, grace, and yes, even a joke or two on the less-than-perfect days.

Before you think this chapter sounds idealistic, hear me out. Sometimes, you'll need to have an extra shot of patience with your coffee before facing another frustrating morning. Don't beat yourself up when you drop the ball or miss a cheer moment. God's grace is abundant. He fills in the gaps. On the flip side, remind yourself that your husband, great as he may be, isn't perfect either. Coaches don't demand flawless players. Cheerleaders don't inspire by berating. We're in this together, flaws and all.

Practical Tips to Get Started

Pray over your role. Before your feet even hit the ground in the morning. Ask God to help you be the encourager and guide your husband needs.
Speak positivity. Every single day actively choose to compliment and affirm your husband at least once daily.
Hold onto humor. Laugh at the small stuff, and don't take life too seriously!
Be his biggest fan. When he accomplishes something—no matter how small—celebrate with a heart full of gratitude.
Forgive freely. Living in Christ means extending grace, even when it's hard.

At the end of the day, being your husband's coach and cheerleader isn't a burden. It is, in fact, one of the greatest blessings of marriage. It can certainly be challenging. Some days might feel like you're calling the plays and hyping the crowd while simultaneously refereeing a chaotic game. But through it all, remember this truth—God called you to this role. He equipped you to be the voice of wisdom, love, and encouragement that your husband needs. You don't have to have all the answers; lean into Him as your ultimate coach. And if all else fails, don't be afraid to hand him the Gatorade (or coffee) and show him your best cheerleader cartwheel. It's all about Him, and it's worth every single play.

Now, I know what you're thinking—what if my marriage is in a tough place right now? What if my husband isn't acting like a team player? Maybe he's distant, frustrated, or carrying resentment. How can I possibly cheer someone on when he is letting me down?

First, take it to God. Ask Him to give you grace, patience, and wisdom. Remember, you're not doing this in your own strength. Philippians 4:13 promises, *"I can do all this through Him who gives me strength."* Lean on that truth, especially when you feel like you've got nothing left to give. Second, realize that your role as a coach and cheerleader doesn't mean you're responsible for fixing your husband. His growth is ultimately between him and God. Your job isn't to take charge of his spiritual progress, it's to support and encourage him along the way. And lastly, stay consistent. Cheerleading is a game of endurance. You won't always see immediate change or recognition, but the seeds of encouragement you plant today may grow into something beautiful down the road. Here's the bottom line—you're not just a wife. You're a God-ordained coach and cheerleader in your husband's life. That's an incredible role, filled with divine purpose and eternal impact. When you love, respect, and uplift him, you're not just strengthening your marriage—you're building a legacy of faith. Marriage is a team sport. Some days, you're going to feel like a Super Bowl-winning coach. Other days, you might feel like you're a failure. But remember this—God is always with you. He's the ultimate coach, encouraging you, equipping you, and cheering you on every step of the way.

Lean into Him, and watch as He transforms your marriage into something only He could design.

Now, go grab those pompoms (metaphorically speaking!) and start cheering for your husband. You've got this—and so does he. There are days when your husband needs you to be his supporter. To be the person who picks him up when his world is crumbling around him. Part of your role in the marriage will always be to cheer and encourage your husband. He must be able to count upon you regardless of what people are saying or who is against him. Your husband is looking for someone behind the scenes (or in the locker room) to compliment him and tell him you are counting on him. Men, although contrary to the opinion of some, often have enormous egos that must be managed. (LOL) While the role of a cheerleader in a marriage is to encourage and offer continuous vocal support, the role of a cheerleader is to ensure your husband stays motivated.

Have you ever been to a function when you hear a person say some negative things about their husband that are not very flattering, followed up with, *I was just kidding?* There are times when he needs someone beside him that he trusts, someone who builds him up in public as well as in private.

Your husband's friends, family, and children are all his cheerleaders. They want him to succeed because they love him and believe in him, giving him a bottomless support. Your husband is often humbled by the outpouring of support he receives from this group. Unfortunately, he will find that this support he receives from outside the family will only go so far. Soon, he will face decisions with real consequences, and he will need a different point of view. He will need someone to disagree with him. Sometimes, we just need someone who will listen and show empathy. He also desperately needs a coach who will be around him for the entire journey. During his dark days, and there will be dark days, you are the person who will make it easier to deal with the darkness. You are the person who will always help him remember what is essential, and it is often very different from what the world is saying. You will be honest with him. Your husband needs someone to tell him when he may be off track and encourage him to look at the harsh truth that he may not see. Coaches support you when you struggle but push you to be better. They celebrate your successes and help you learn from your failures. More than anything else, they are honest with you, even if it tells you something you do not want to hear.

It might be interesting to hear some comments from real guys regarding how they wish their wives would help build them up. Some of these suggestions involve Coaching, and some include being his cheerleader. Before the ideas listed below, your first and foremost role is loving and respecting your husband by putting Jesus first. You cannot love him without the love of God. With God at the center, you can build your husband up in many ways!

How we love each other should be a picture of God's love. God loves us by building us up. He loves us; therefore, we should build each other up, not put each other down. When he feels respected and wanted, he goes out of the way to do those little things you desire. Although we fall short, with Jesus in the middle of your marriage, we can build each other up. A man who knows his wife has confidence in him and can move mountains. Your encouragement can help your husband step into his calling. It can encourage him to be the best he can be. You have the power to speak life into your husband. You can build him up. We are called to build, and by building, you show him respect, which he so longs for from you. A man's damaged ego is often tricky to repair. After all, you are the person he promised he would honor, protect, and live together with forever. You are the person he committed to taking care of when you were sick and old. It was only a few years ago that you and your husband agreed in front of all our friends and especially God that we were going to be one.

I am sure your husband has many flaws. He may not still be the sex symbol you married. He has perhaps expanded around the midsection and is not as big of a hardbody as he once was. One of the best ways to see the return of the guy you married is to treat him like you did when you were courting. Brag on him and tell him how great he is and what a great father and husband he is. You will soon see him begin to respond and behave as you treat him.

CHAPTER 7

MARRIAGE IS FOR GROWN-UPS

Just the word marriage stirs up an array of emotions and images, some of fairy-tale romance and others, well, not so much. You probably walked into marriage a bit starry-eyed, holding onto dreams of breakfast in bed, uninterrupted Hallmark dates, and maybe even someone who would agree to take out the trash without being nudged. Then reality hits and He's leaving his socks in the living room again, for the seventh time. That's because marriage, is no walk in the park. But here's the good news: it's not supposed to be easy. Marriage is for adults. It's for grown-ups. And honestly? There's no better boot camp for spiritual growth, humility, and love than joining lives with another imperfect human being under the same roof.

When we say that marriage is for grown-ups, we're not just talking about turning 18 and signing a marriage license. We mean spiritual, emotional, and relational maturity, the kind that makes you look at an argument over an unclosed toothpaste cap and laugh instead of launching into a *third world war level* silent treatment. It's the kind of growth where you learn to recognize the plank in your own eye before pointing out the speck in your husband's eye (Matthew 7:3). Trust me, this is one spiritual workout that will have you flexing humility and patience muscles you didn't even know you had. But there's also beauty in the mess. Think of marriage as God's tool for refining us—like gold in fire. Except sometimes, that fire feels less like the gentle warmth of a Sunday sermon and more like being roasted alive in a coffee roaster. Marriage will push you, stretch you, and yes, even exhaust you, but every moment spent ironing out those wrinkles is a moment closer to reflecting God's design for love. Remember, this isn't only about surviving marriage—it's about thriving and growing into the likeness of Christ.

Now, before we go off into some poetic description of love, dripping with all the wrong kinds of syrupy sweetness, let's laugh at some truths. Real, raw, unfiltered truths. Take prayer, for example. You know you're a grown-up in marriage when instead of praying for your husband to be less annoying, you start praying for wisdom and compassion to meet him with grace on the days he's feeling distant or stressed. That's the holy pivot. That's what separates the wheat from the chaff.

And let's talk forgiveness—real, relentless forgiveness. Not the dramatic kind you see in movies with swelling orchestral music but the raw, 6 a.m., *I forgive you for forgetting to buy milk like I asked* kind of forgiveness. Because here's the thing —when you forgive your husband, even in the mundane, you mirror God's forgiving heart toward us. How many times has God forgiven you for every unspoken *sock in the living room* scenario played out in our spiritual lives? Too many to count. Forgiveness is for the strong. Forgiveness is for the grown-ups and it's a non-negotiable in marriage. Love keeps no record of wrongs. Well, that includes forgetting that time he forgot your birthday or forgot your parent's anniversary.

And when we talk about sacrificial love, we'd be remiss if we didn't give a shoutout to the silent saints of *I'll take the kids while you nap* moments and *I won't comment on the ironing when you do it kind of wrinkly* offerings. These moments may seem small, but they are the building blocks of a marriage fueled by grace. It's not all spiritual growth and heavenly skies. Cupboards slam, voices get raised, and nights occasionally end with one of you sleeping on the edge of the bed, facing the opposite direction, of course. These moments don't make you bad at marriage; they make you a human in marriage. Paul didn't say "*Love is patient*" because love naturally is patient; he said it because he knew it needs to be. That's why God is at the center of this whole thing. You can't do it in your own strength, and honestly, why would you? Marriage was designed to pull you both closer to each other and closer to Him.

On your wedding day, you and your husband promised to be faithful to each other "*for better, for worse, for richer, for poorer, in sickness and in health, until death does us part.*" Often, however, many couples face the worse or poorer or sickness in their marriage—because marriage is hard work. When my children were planning their weddings, I thought long and hard about what advice I should give them before their big day. All sorts of ideas came to mind; however, one idea continued to present itself to me. The primary advice I came up with was, *Marriage is hard work; marriage is for grown-ups.* I know this was different from what they were anticipating hearing. They probably thought I would bestow upon them some profound physiological concept about the bonds of holy matrimony. But the most honest advice I could give was that marriage can be complicated—sometimes very hard, even if both the husband and wife are trying. My children were looking to me for inspiration, and I must have sounded like I was trying to talk them out of getting married. All of my children have now been married for a minimum of five years, and if asked, they would say I was correct at least about one thing in my life—marriage is challenging but well worth the investment. I knew each of my children well, and I could see they were doing as I had done, idealizing marriage as they wanted it to be.

There are two common reasons marriage is for grown-ups. First, you and your husband may discover you are challenging to live with. You are a neat freak; he never picks up his clothes. You like to rise early; he enjoys staying up late. You want intimate snuggling and cuddling; he loves sex.

Husbands and wives also discover that although they dated for a long time, they didn't realize how different their personalities were. It is easy for both of you to assume that once married, the other would make the necessary changes to create perfect harmony in the marriage. As you were married, you began to see how different this person was from who you thought you were marring. It might have something to do with the fact that you're both accustomed to understanding your needs as the most critical issue you had to deal with, and now you have someone else that has to be added to the mix. You may insist on having your way far more than you realize.

The single most significant thing that will make your marriage hard is the failure to let go of your sometimes unreal expectations of your husband. You've got a laundry list of qualities you expected in him, and good news, he will have some of those qualities. But he will also bring faults and character issues into the marriage, and dealing with those will test the limits of your patience. Marriage is like moving into a house built by two very different architects. One wants sleek modern lines and a minimalist approach; the other dreams of a cozy cottage with warm lighting. Yet, despite their differences, these architects unite under one roof, vowing to make it work through love, sweat, and divine guidance. That, my friends, is marriage—a union so beautiful, yet so complex, it could only be designed by the Creator Himself.

Marriage is, in every sense of the word, for grown-ups. Before you bristle at the implication, let's clarify what that means. It's not about a specific age, level of income, or number of gray hairs. No, being a grown-up in marriage is about maturity: emotional, spiritual, and sometimes even the patience kind of maturity that tells you to hold your tongue.

Marriage will test your ability to forgive—truly forgive, not just give the *Yeah, okay, let's move past this* mumble only to bring it up in a new argument two weeks later. Forgiveness isn't for the faint of heart. It's heavy lifting, spiritually and emotionally, and sometimes it means owning your part in the conflict. That's right, grown-ups in marriage need to admit when they're wrong. And I'm not talking about a begrudging *fine, you win* statement. I'm talking about sincere, honest accountability. Our Savior himself modeled forgiveness in a way that leaves even the most mature among us humbled. He bore the greatest offense, the most unimaginable betrayal, and still forgave. If we are called to reflect His love in our marriages, then forgiveness is not optional.

Does this mean marriage is about gritting your teeth through unbearable situations? Absolutely not. Healthy boundaries, mutual respect, and God-centered love must always remain foundational. Forgiveness must flow from those principles, not replace them. Here's another maturity speed bump we all face in marriage—our human need for reciprocity. Marriage maturity throws that out the window and says, *I'll love and serve even if it feels like I'm doing more today.*

Jesus showed us this when He washed the feet of His disciples. Think about that. The most important, holiest figure in the room humbled Himself to serve. That's the model for how we're to treat our spouses—not as servants or caretakers, but as selfless partners. Serving your spouse can look like making them breakfast, buying them a thoughtful gift, or holding back an *I told you so* when they've clearly lost their car keys for the third time this week. Marriage isn't about scoring points; it's about building a relationship founded on unshakable love.

Maturity in marriage comes from a shared commitment to your faith. When couples seek God together, they strengthen their relationship on the most solid foundation possible. It's in prayer, worship, and studying the Word together that you'll find the growth you could never achieve individually. Your husband's spiritual maturity sets the tone for your family. Your wisdom and discernment can be a gift to your husband's understanding of biblical truth. Together, you sharpen one another and model faith for the next generation.

Marriage is an adventure that begins with a promise and continues with intentional choices—many of which require you both to grow beyond your comfort zones. The good news is that God, in His immense wisdom and grace, equips us for this lifelong partnership. He doesn't call you to perfection but to reliance on Him. Your marriage is a testimony. It's a living, breathing reflection of Christ's love story with the church. And if you're feeling overwhelmed, if forgiveness feels hard —take heart in knowing you're not alone. God's design for marriage is not just for grown-ups—it's for *His* grown-ups, who are still learning, still growing, and most importantly, still loved.

Time has a way of slowly changing many things. If you remember, there was a time when you both were giddy and in love. You couldn't believe that anything would ever go awry between you. Creating a lasting marriage is a humbling experience. It is part skill, luck, elbow grease, and blind determination. All couples experience hills and valleys, yet predictable transitional periods are often misunderstood, causing overreactions. Those who weather these stormy periods usually have greater love and commitment to each other. Though all marriages are unique and all unions are hard, most marriages experience predictable stages. One of America's most outstanding experts and best-selling authors on marriage is *Michele Weiner-Davis*. She is the founder of the *Divorce Busting* consulting group and *The Place Where Marriages Become Stronger and More Committed*. She highlights the different stages that most marriages pass through.

Phase One: Passion typically fills the first stage of marriage. Starry-eyed in love with your husband, you finish each other's sentences and usually overlook annoying things. At no other time in your relationship is your feeling of well-being and physical desire for each other as intense. The newness and excitement of the relationship stimulate the production of chemicals in your body that increase energy and positive attitudes and heighten sexuality and sensuality.

Stage Two. This is when reality sets in. Little things bother you, like stinky breath in the morning, toilet seats left up, stuff strewn on the counter, and forgetting to pay bills. You argue a lot and keep reminding yourself you made a lifelong commitment. While feeling at odds with your once-kindred spirit, you are faced with making life-altering decisions. Should we have children? Where should we live? Who will support the family, who will pay the bills, and who will do the cooking? Spouses often start to feel like members of opposing teams.

Stage Three. At this point, most people believe there are two ways of looking at things: your way and your husband's. Couples battle to get their partner to admit they are wrong. Every disagreement is an opportunity to define the marriage. Both partners dig in their heels. Convinced they've tried everything, many couples give up, telling themselves they've fallen out of love or married the wrong person. Other people resign themselves to the situation and lead separate lives together. Still, others decide it's time to investigate healthier, more satisfying interaction methods. Requiring a significant leap of faith, those who take it are the fortunate ones because the best of marriage is yet to come.

Stage Four. Couples realize seeing eye-to-eye on everything is unlikely. They work to live more peaceably. They seek wise counsel from close friends and family and marriage seminars or counseling. "Hardheadedness" is more comfortable and forgiving as each person recognizes that neither party is easy to live with. When disagreements occur, couples try to put themselves in each other's shoes more often. They realize they have to accept the good and the bad. Fights happen less frequently and are less intense or emotional than before.

Stage Five. Many couples never get to this stage. No longer struggling to define what the marriage should be, there is more peace and harmony. You start liking your spouse again. While both agree marriage hasn't been easy, there is shared history, and you feel proud you've weathered the storms. You appreciate your partner's sense of commitment to making your marriage last. You begin to appreciate the differences between you and your husband. What you don't enjoy, you find greater acceptance for. You realize you have come full circle.

Marriage seems easy before you do it, but obstacles can quickly get in the way. It is hard for you, and it is hard for your husband. God knew it was going to be hard, but when we bring in your parents and extended families, it skyrockets to a new level. Have you ever said, *That is not how my daddy did it*, or, *My daddy said……?* And, have you also heard in return, *I am not your daddy!* You probably believe your dad is the most incredible man on earth. However, what may surprise your husband is how deep the bond between you and your father can be, how powerful it remains throughout your life, and how resilient it can be.

My wife's father passed away before we were married, so I didn't have to deal with this conflict as much as some men, but I had to deal with something just as frustrating. No matter what happens in our lives, my wife suggests I call my dad anytime anything goes wrong. She believed that he could fix anything, and quite frankly, he could. As a new husband, I was not very helpful with things around the house; however, I wanted to make sure my wife knew that the guy she married was totally clueless. We needed a fresh start, where we had to depend on each other.

This does not suggest that you and your parents should cut off all relations. But your primary human relationship now is with your husband, not your parents. Your commitment to God comes first, followed by your bond to your husband, your children, your family of origin, and your extended family and friends. Parents and their married children can sometimes have difficulty with the balance between the concepts of "*leave and cleave*" and "honoring parents."

Many marriages fail because of interference from outsiders. For a marriage to work, the spouse needs to loosen her ties with the family of origin and forge new ones with the new family she creates through marriage. This doesn't mean she can't have a close relationship with their extended families, but she needs to set proper boundaries with them to ensure that her spouse has first priority in her life.

There will come a time in your marriage when you and your husband will identify behaviors that seem to put you at odds and maybe even drive you a bit crazy. Hopefully, you and your husband are at the point where you refuse to argue over the small, insignificant stuff of life. If we think back, what are the things we disagree on? They are not usually life-changing discussions or ideas that are the least bit important to your marriage or your family. Silly things that grown-ups can walk away from. Your marriage will become much more comfortable once you reach this imaginary place where you know how to avoid an argument. When you are young, you may have done things that purposely frustrated your husband, who did the same thing to you. Hopefully, you have reached the point where you feel too grown up for silly, immature behaviors. If so, you will agree that there are behaviors that mature adults can adopt in their marriage and stop having the childish squabbles of the past.

Marriage is challenging, yet it is worth the trouble. Why do couples give it up and decide to be unfaithful to their mate? There are many reasons; however, none are acceptable. Is the grass greener on the other side of the fence? Is it because everybody is doing it? Is it due to how socially acceptable it appears to be?

Some marriages struggle from the get-go and wonder why it's so hard, but the good news is that there will be more to your marriage than struggling. You'll play together, pray for each other, comfort one another in sorrow, and make each other laugh. So don't worry: You will love each other despite your frustrations.

Finally, remember that you're not just growing up for yourselves; you're growing up for each other. The Bible says, *"Two are better than one… If either of them falls down, one can help the other up"* (Ecclesiastes 4:9-10). Your husband is your partner in this life, not your opponent. God brought you together to glorify Him, to reflect His love in your home and outward to the world. Marriage is for grown-ups—spiritually, emotionally, and yes, occasionally humorously. It's less about chasing perfection and more about choosing each other daily, even on the tough days. You're going to mess up. You're going to grow. And in the end, you're going to see God's faithfulness in ways you couldn't have imagined.

CHAPTER 8

DATING YOUR HUSBAND THE OLD WAY

No kids.
No bedtimes.
No discipline.
No being mommy.
No washing dishes.
No cooking dinner.

When was the last time you went on a real date with your husband? And no, running errands together on a Saturday morning or sitting side by side on your phones while Netflix hums in the background doesn't count. If you're racking your brain and coming up with nothing, don't feel bad. Life happens. Kids, jobs, church activities, laundry piles that could probably qualify as a small mountain range—all of it demands our attention in ways that push romantic gestures to the very bottom of the priority list. But here's the thing, just because you said *I do* doesn't mean the pursuit ends.

Marriage doesn't come with an autopilot mode, where you throw on a wedding ring and magically coast to *happily ever after*. It takes intentionality, deliberate action, and yes, a healthy dose of humor. Because let's face it—marriage can be one of the most beautiful but also downright awkward things God designed for us.

But here's what we know from scripture. God created marriage as a reflection of Christ's love for us. Ephesians 5:25 calls husbands to love their wives just as Christ loved the church and gave himself up for her. That's a big deal. And while that verse is often aimed at the men, wives carry a huge opportunity in marriage too—to nurture, to honor, and to keep the flame alive. Dating your husband isn't just a nice idea; it's an investment in one of life's most sacred relationships.

Before your wedding day, chances are you put serious effort into dating. Hours searching for the perfect date outfit. Nerves building up before he picked you up at your parents' house. Butterflies fluttering in your stomach when your hands brushed during a drive. But now? The butterflies somehow morphed into boring budget discussions and the occasional argument about dishwasher loading strategies.

Dating your husband isn't about re-creating your early days. It's about intentionally creating new moments of connection. Why? Because love craves attention. Neglecting your marriage—even unintentionally—can quickly create distance. And who wants that? Marriage is meant to thrive, not just survive. But more importantly, investing in your husband reminds him of something crucial—that he is seen, valued, and fiercely loved. It's incredible what affirmation through connection can do for a man's heart.

Marriage is a beautiful union, divinely ordained, but let's be real—it's not always sunshine and roses. Between work, kids, schedules that look like a battlefield, and laundry piles that could double as Mount Sinai, romance often falls somewhere between *If I have time* and *Is that even a thing anymore?* And yet, when you said *I do*, you didn't just sign up for mundane routines; you vowed to cherish, love, and honor each other—through all seasons of life, even the messy ones. But what if I told you that the secret to breathing fresh life into your marriage isn't found in some elaborate grand gesture? What if it's not about picture-perfect Instagram dates or a tropical vacation that requires a second mortgage? Sometimes, the secret isn't new at all. Sometimes, the key is going back to falling in love the old way.

Yes, I'm talking about dating your husband. Not in the way society shouts at us, but in the raw, authentic, old-school way. If your marriage is like a triangle, God is at the top, and you and your husband occupy the bottom corners. The closer you both climb toward Him, the closer you'll naturally draw to each other. When was the last time you prayed for and with your husband? Not just asking God to keep him from snacking at 11 PM, but genuine prayers that align your hearts with God's? Prayer is the ultimate act of intimacy, binding two souls at a spiritual level far richer than anything on this earth. Philippians 2:3-4 reminds us to value others above ourselves, not looking *"to our own interests but each of you to the interests of the others."* How often do you think about how your husband feels loved and valued? He deeply desires your respect, your genuine attention, and yes, probably even your laughter when he's telling that same goofy joke for the fifth time.

Do you remember that giddy, puppy-love laugh you used to have when dating? Back when you were still trying to impress each other, every shared joke became the funniest thing in the world. Where did that laughter go? Did it get buried under overdue bills or carpooling schedules? It's time to dig it out. Laughter is one of the simplest gifts God gave us in marriage. Proverbs 17:22 says, *"A cheerful heart is good medicine..."* Your marriage will be healthier and more joy-filled the moment you choose to laugh together. Whether it's a shared inside joke, a hilarious mishap around the house, or reminiscing about old memories, humor brings light into the mundane. Next time something small goes wrong—like burning dinner or your toddler streaking through the Zoom call your husband was presenting—choose laughter over frustration. Life's too short not to find joy tucked in the little absurdities.

Do you remember when dating meant dressing up just to walk through Walmart together? Or when sharing a milkshake felt like the height of romance? Why do we abandon that simplicity now? Dating doesn't have to be elaborate— sometimes, the old ways are the best ways. Hand-written notes, impromptu walks around the neighborhood, or even swinging by his office with his favorite coffee can spark the kind of connection you yearn for.

No marriage is perfect—no date will be, either. Maybe your plans get rained out, your budget doesn't allow for fancy dinners, or babysitters feel harder to come by than world peace. That's okay. Marriage isn't sustained by perfectly choreographed moments; it thrives in the imperfections when you choose each other, regardless. Dancing in the rain might seem cliché, but trust me—whether it's literal or figurative rain, you can dance through it. It's about finding joy in the midst of chaos. Maybe your date night ends with both of you asleep on the couch halfway through a movie. But you tried—that effort alone matters more than you realize.

The beauty of marriage isn't in its destination. Just like our faith, it's in the day-by-day process of choosing love—messy, uninspired, full-of-laundry love—over convenience. Imagine how God smiles when He sees us lifting each other up within our vows, not out of obligation, but out of devotion. Hebrews 10:24-25 says, *"And let us consider how we may spur one another on toward love and good deeds, not giving up meeting together…"* Dating your husband even now is an act of meeting together—not giving up on the spark God ignited in your union. Who says old-school romance can't thrive in a Netflix-subscription world? Take it from Ecclesiastes 4:9—*"Two are better than one, because they have a good reward for their labor."* Whether that *"reward"* is rekindled love or simply a cheeseburger at 11 PM, it's worth every effort. Now toss on your sneakers, hold his hand unashamedly, and go love him like you're trying to win him over all over again. Because isn't he worth it?

Date night can be a relaxing and enjoyable time for you and your husband. It is a time that you both look forward to, as it will often take you back to your dating days. You both must follow several rules to make these incredible evenings worthwhile. Just think for a minute. Do you remember how much fun it was when you two could go out with each other, hang out, laugh, talk, and maybe even eat without interruption? The times you laughed, even when his stories weren't hilarious, shared slightly embellished stories from your past, and ended the night by doing a lot of touching, snuggling, and whispering. Nothing in the world seemed to matter other than being with the man you loved. You clung to every word he spoke, and the closest you came to solving a real problem was deciding where and what you would eat for dinner.

You are to behave like you are still dating each other. Otherwise, what you are planning is not a date night but rather just a night out when the kids stay home. That is a very different concept! Routine is easy to do, but it is the shortcut to stagnation. You don't have to look far to see marriages that have stagnated. Things were much more comfortable early in your marriage or when you were dating. With no children, few real responsibilities, and a more toned body— you only had to make minor adjustments and enhancements before going out, but nothing was a big deal. Now, date night has a whole different meaning. Before having a date night, there is so much you have to accomplish before the event. There is so much to do that it is often not worth the effort, so you and your husband make the events less and less frequent. The purpose of the evening is to have fun, chill, and enjoy each other. Now you're married, and a free night out doesn't come along very often unless you prioritize it. Instead of just walking out the door, it can usually be a big deal.

Do you remember your dating days. The times that you felt like you had arrived at the Promised Land: The hot date. You had been thinking nonstop about this handsome guy you met for weeks and liked what you saw. You had been flirting as hard as you could, and he was playing hard to get with all his might. No matter how you sliced it, you were head over heels with this guy, and he was willing to give you a chance to be the only girl he kissed for the foreseeable future. There was no test in college that you prepared for more than one of our dates.

Date after date, you tried to make the next date better than the first. You decided to assess every possible fun date idea and carefully select the right one. You wanted to know if you had picked the right movie to see. You wondered what he would wanted to eat, knowing that it had to be reasonably priced. You wondered what you should talk about that would be fun and, at the same time, impress him that he was the one you had been looking for.

Getting ready for a date on which you wanted to impress your future husband was a lot to keep track of. You found that many of the essential things when you were first dating are also important now that you have date night with each other. You must be prepared. You must be prepared and take these nights seriously, and your husband must follow suit.

To maximize your time and shared experiences, you should consider the following suggestions or make your own:

Get Yourself Ready: Make going on your date a big deal. Clean up and wash away your workday. Brush your teeth, dump the bad breath, fix your hair and makeup, and look like you are trying to get another date with this hot dude who is now your husband. Just walking out the door with no preparation is telling your husband that this is a night you don't have to cook, but don't get any ideas about anything else.

Look Good. Whether you care for fashion or not, remember that your clothing is a form of nonverbal communication, and it also forms part of your husband's impression of how excited you are to be going out with him. Make sure you dress the way your husband likes you to look. Looking good will reap confidence benefits if you feel great about the way you look.

Be Pleasant. Smile when you are getting ready at home and smile during the date. Avoid controversial conversations and topics that may possibly be a downer for you or your husband. Agree upfront to leave kids, work, finances, and problems at home out of the conversation.

Work At The Date. Many times, people who have been married for a long time end up with nothing to talk about. It sounds wild, but it is true. What can sometimes follow is awkward silence, and your mind starts wondering about everything you must do when you get home. Have 3-5 questions prepared that can serve as a conversation starter. Talking about pleasant things in your past is a great place to start. That way, you can relax and know that you are prepared.

Give Yourself A Motivational Talk. Get excited about going out. It is effortless to leave your mind on auto-pilot when getting ready and begin to worry about children, how you look, finances, and other things. Put it out of your mind and get fired up for the night. Don't start.

Regularity. How often are you going to have a night out? If you plan the night out, it will happen. The nights become fewer and fewer, and you even start counting a drive-thru on the way home from a soccer game as your night out and scraping out a date night once every three months will take a lot of work. It would help if you made time regularly and consistently to enjoy alone time. How many children you have, what ages they are, who can keep them, and the cost must be factored in regarding the frequency of your night.

Variety. What do you usually do when you have a date night? Doing the same thing or going to the same place over and over can become monotonous. This is true in every area of life. What once was fun and refreshing can become a mere routine. So spice up your couple time with a wide range of exciting pursuits. The decision of what to do or where to go shouldn't be a burden. It should be a trade-off so neither you nor your husband feels pressured to decide and plan the night.

Adventure. You don't have to become a party planner to introduce a sense of adventure into your time together. You also don't have to plan something elaborate or expensive, either. Maintaining a sense of adventure means merely including new, unusual, or unexpected elements.

Fun. When was the last time you laughed hysterically at each other? Having fun might seem obvious, but it's more important than you realize. Research shows that couples who engage in fun activities together enjoy deeper intimacy. So, whatever you do during your date night and other moments when you're enjoying leisure time as a couple, make sure it's FUN!

Your marriage is not all fun and games. You know that is often the myth we chase when trying to keep up with today's culture. Building your relationship on mutually enjoyable experiences will leave you better equipped to weather the storms when they come. Always approaching date night as though you're trying to get a second date can be essential! We sometimes forget that we must pursue and "woo" our husbands. So, spruce it up a bit. Smile, talk about him, brag about him, act as though you are the luckiest woman alive. Be affectionate – hold hands, cuddle, and steal kisses.

Dating your spouse cultivates delayed gratification. If you read any advice column about how to keep the spark alive in your marriage, you will find date night near the top of the list. Yet, if you are like most couples, you'll read it, note it, and ignore it. Dating and marriage seem like a contradiction. When couples try to spend time together and continue developing their relationship, no matter what's going on in their everyday life, they are more likely to grow closer rather than apart.

In the busyness of life and raising your families, your marriage risks going underwater as you seek to meet everyone's expectations. Your dates don't have to look like the Joneses, but don't go to the other extreme and forget about them, either. Your marriage will be strengthened and helped as you spend intentional time together, honoring the spouse God has given you to share life with. It's not what you do; it's the spirit you bring to it. Sometimes, our date night consisted of putting the kids to bed and sitting in the backyard on lawn chairs, watching for shooting stars.

Attempting to date your husband doesn't mean you'll magically erase every marital hiccup. Sometimes you'll schedule a romantic evening, only for your toddler to wake up screaming "MOMMMMY!" halfway through dessert. Sometimes he'll be distracted by work or you'll get into a mini argument over whose turn it is to do bedtime. That's real life. But don't give up. Keep pursuing. Keep trying. Because love is less about grand perfection and more about faithful action. God designed your marriage to be strengthened through commitment, even when it's messy. Ecclesiastes 4:9-10 reminds us, "*Two are better than one, because they have a good return for their labor. If either falls down, one can help the other up.*" Life is unpredictable. But choosing to date your husband—even in the mundane moments—is a choice to keep laying bricks that build a stronger, God-honoring foundation.

Married life is crazy, beautiful, exhausting, hilarious, and sacred all rolled into one. But dating your husband isn't about adding more to your to-do list. It's about nourishing a relationship that God designed to be life-giving—for both of you. Imagine what could happen if every Christian marriage had spouses that actively pursued one another. A world where love layered with laughter and faith was the norm. That's the heartbeat of God's vision for marriage. You're not alone in this journey The Bible provides your roadmap, your community surrounds you, and God's love sustains your effort. No matter how long you've been married, there's no better day to start dating your husband than today. And who knows? You might just rediscover why you fell for him in the first place. Now, go grab his hand and plan that date—cheesy pickup line optional but highly recommended.

CHAPTER 9

ACTIONS SPEAK LOUDER THAN WORDS

Picture this. It's a Saturday morning, the perfect kind for pancakes. You're leaning over the counter, flipping those golden beauties, while your husband sits cozied up on the couch binging his favorite sports highlights. You're thinking to yourself, *Well, wouldn't it be nice if he offered to lend a hand?* Instead, you get a playful commentary about your flipping technique. Marriage is a complex, beautiful, extraordinary gift from God... and yes, sometimes, it's a bit of a workout. It's like building a house together. Love? That's the foundation. Communication? The walls that keep everything standing. And actions? Well, they're those finishing touches—the coat of paint, the flowers on the windowsills. Beautiful words may get the house noticed, but it's what you do that keeps it a home.

We all know the saying *actions speak louder than words*, but have you thought about how this saying plays out in marriage? Stick with me here. You can tell your husband I love you a thousand times a day, but if right after that you roll your eyes over his choice in socks or criticize every little thing he does—you're sending a pretty confusing message, right? Trust me; I've been guilty of this too. *But love isn't a checklist of to-dos*, I hear you protest. And you're absolutely right—it isn't. But love does look a lot like work, sometimes in very intentional ways.

Think for a moment about Christ's love for us. Did He merely say He loved us? No. He demonstrated it through His actions, right to the cross. Ephesians 5 tells us that husbands are to love their wives as Christ loved the church. And ladies, that example works both ways. While we were called to submit to our husbands, we balance that with the commitment to love, cherish, and honor them, just as Christ shows His love for us through service and sacrifice. It's easier to say, *You're my everything*, but harder to follow that up by joyfully engaging in the mundane—packing lunches, carpool duty, folding that mountain of laundry sitting in the basket for the past week— or graciously biting your tongue when you're tempted to throw a sarcastic zinger his way in a moment of frustration.

More often than not, our kindness prompts kindness in return. When you go out of your way to show love—even in the moments when you don't feel like it—he notices. And sure, it might not always click right away, but love doesn't keep a scorecard. Actions speak to the heart—it's the way God wired us.And okay, real talk—what about the irritating stuff? What about those quirks that make you want to roll your eyes out loud? Maybe he leaves cereal boxes open like it's a sport, zones out mid-conversation, or stashes gum wrappers in the couch cushions. The truth is, some days you might feel like sending those quirks straight to the moon.

But grace, is where we shine God's love in those moments. Remember Colossians 3:13, *"Bear with each other and forgive one another if any of you has a grievance against someone. Forgive as the Lord forgave you.*" It's humbling, isn't it? When we show grace—by choosing patient action over sharp criticism—we reflect Christ. That doesn't mean bottling up frustrations or avoiding honest conversations about things that matter. Communication is vital. But there's a difference between addressing a genuine issue and nit-picking over things that hold little weight.

Marriage, in many ways, is like a grand symphony, filled with crescendos of joy, moments of quiet reflection, and yes, the occasional discordant note. But as every good musician knows, even the best symphonies require practice, dedication, and the willingness to tune out the noise to focus on what matters most. For Christian couples, marriage is more than just a shared life—it's a covenant, a reflection of God's love for us. And while words matter—"I love you" and promises of devotion hold a sacred place in our hearts—our daily actions are what bring those words to life. If you've been married for more than five minutes, you've probably realized that marriage isn't all rainbows and butterflies. It's also overflowing trash cans, laundry piles that seem to multiply on their own, and the eternal question, *What's for dinner?* Sometimes, the temptation is to rely on words to smooth things over. But as the saying goes, *actions speak louder than words.*

This book is not about assigning blame or keeping score—it's a call for both spouses to lean into the daily acts of love that sustain a marriage. It's about aligning your actions with God's purpose for your relationship and ensuring those actions echo His love. James 1:22 reminds us, *"Do not merely listen to the word, and so deceive yourselves. Do what it says."* While this passage encourages us in our spiritual lives, it holds just as much power in our marriages. Listening and speaking are important, but action—living out the Word—is where transformation happens.

Small gestures like folding the laundry without being asked, planning a thoughtful date night, or even simply turning off your phone to listen can speak love far louder than words can. Think of these gestures as deposits into your relational bank account—every choice, no matter how seemingly mundane, plays into the bigger picture of love and commitment. Stop and think about how God shows His love for us. Sure, we have His Word, but God didn't stop at spoken promises. His love was demonstrated through action—most profoundly in the sacrifice of Jesus Christ. Romans 5:8 spells it out perfectly, *"But God demonstrates his own love for us in this: While we were still sinners, Christ died for us."*

God didn't just tell us He loved us; He showed us. And as Christians, we're called to model His love in every aspect of our lives, including our marriages. When you serve your spouse selflessly, even in the small ways—making coffee in the morning, leaving a sweet note, or tackling the chore you know they dread—you're reflecting the love Christ has for us. It's not always easy, mind you. Sometimes, serving in love means doing something for your spouse even when you don't particularly feel like it. But isn't that what sacrificial love is all about?

When your husband lets you down—and he will, because no one is perfect—choose forgiveness. Not begrudging forgiveness that comes with a side of passive-aggressiveness, but genuine, Christlike forgiveness. And forgiveness, by the way, isn't just an emotional state. It's an action. It's choosing not to hold a grudge, choosing to move forward, and choosing to show love even when it's hard.

Perhaps the greatest question we can ask ourselves each day is, *How can I love my spouse better today?* Maybe that love looks like making an extra effort to express your appreciation through a kind word and a thoughtful action. Maybe it's being more present during conversations, putting the phone on airplane mode to eliminate distractions. Or maybe it's something as simple as offering a hug at the end of a long, exhausting day.

Whatever form your love takes, remember this—your actions don't go unnoticed. They build, piece by piece, the type of marriage that glorifies God and blesses your lives together. To every Christian couple reading, know this: Marriage isn't about perfection. It's about progress. Each small, love-filled action adds up to a lifetime of shared joy, deep trust, and unwavering partnership. Yes, words have power, but actions? Actions have lasting impact.

After I graduated from college, my friend Charles moved to New York City and accepted a position in the New York Public Library System. Like so many new graduates, he started at the bottom; however, after twenty years, he had grown to the Vice President of Operations. It was a tremendous organization, and he held a vital position. After waiting too long, I scheduled a trip and visited him. That's when I discovered that my old friend from a small town in rural Tennessee was now the executive vice president of the entire system, which had thousands and thousands of employees. I was impressed and proud of what this small-town country boy had accomplished. Charles was a person who had no interest in leading and managing people when in college; plus, he was one of the most compassionate people I had ever met.

My first morning in New York City, Charles stopped by my hotel, and we walked to his office in the heart of Midtown. The city was bustling with men and women, each in their own world, practically running down the streets. Human beings were everywhere; none spoke or even looked at the people around them. The dress of the day and every day in New York City was either dark navy, grey, or black. As we slowed at a corner, waiting for the light to change, an older, well-dressed gentleman was waiting to cross the street. Charles tapped him on the shoulder and paid him a nice compliment. Charles looked at his old, falling apart, beat-up briefcase and indicated that he imagined the briefcase was special to him. The man was wearing a thousand-dollar suit and cashmere overcoat and was carrying a briefcase that appeared to be worn out. The man looked at Charles and smiled, *It is special to me. My twin sons gave this to me about 30 years ago as a Father's Day present, and I have never been to the office without it.* He smiled, we smiled, and then we were all off hurrying down the street.

As we passed the busy construction entrance for a new super skyscraper a bulky, rough-looking worker passed us, adjusting his hard hat. He was carrying heavy equipment dangling from his belt and hanging over his shoulder. Charles once again spoke to the stranger and asked him about his job on the construction site. The man indicated he was a steelworker and worked on the top of the 100-story building being constructed. Charles said, *Are you kidding me? I am sure your wife and kids are proud of how brave you are and how dangerous your job is.* The steelworker displayed a brief smile and continued into the construction site, but with a little bit of pep in his step, I observed. I began to see a pattern but was unaware of what was happening. Charles was the only guy in New York City speaking to strangers.

The final straw was seeing a woman walking toward us on the sidewalk. It was the middle of the winter, and she wore a white dress with large multi-colored flowers boldly printed on it. I began to say a little prayer, thinking surely Charles wouldn't say anything to this woman, but he did. Charles walked up to her and smiled, then let her know that he saw her walking down the street as soon as she turned the corner.

He said I couldn't help but notice how beautiful your dress is. He wanted her to know that she made his day. She didn't know how to take the compliment at first, thinking he might be poking fun at her, but soon realized he was authentic..

We finally reached Charles's office, he introduced me around, and then we had some quiet time together. I couldn't wait to ask him what had just happened on our walk downtown, the way he spoke to people and paid them compliments. He nodded and told me his story. *When I moved to New York City years ago, I decided I wanted to let the people of New York City know that I loved them, and I wanted to show it in my actions and not just his words every day.* He told me he often could show his love and care for people easier than he could say to them in such a big city. So he was on a mission every trip to and from the office. He said, *I don't know if this is making any difference, but I chose to believe it is. I hope the man with the briefcase will call his sons and tell them about his encounter and how much he loves them both. I hope the steelworker will go home, hug his kids, and kiss his wife because he realizes they are so proud of him. And the lady with the cool dress, what if she is a schoolteacher? Her kids would be in for a great day with her feeling so good about herself.*

Your husband may be more focused on how he treats others than you. It isn't that he loves them more; it's just that he assumes you know how much he loves you, and he believes that his actions all day will show you that. Your husband often goes out of his way to show you that he loves you; however, he may not verbalize it as much or in the way that you desire. Working hard to provide for you and the family is an authentic way he says, I love you, without using words. Sacrificing his free time to attend all of his kid's practices and games is a way he says I love you to them without using words. He often assumes that actions mean more than words. He knows that behavior is usually not what you desire, but this is frequently how he is wired.

Some men say *I love you* when they really mean, *I think you're wonderful*. Or, *Right now, I am so happy just being with you*. The problem with words for some men, even the most thoughtful and well-written ones, is that when actions do not accompany them, they see them as words that have lost meaning. Men often believe you can't depend on words alone, while you usually think you want to hear love, not just see it. I have heard men say that their wives are so wrapped up in the words they don't mean that they don't appreciate how hard they are working to show their actions. Maybe this is why scripture teaches us that men need to be reminded to *love their wife*, or more clearly, to tell her how much he loves her.

Your husband may believe that love presents itself in actions long after the words have run their course. It may be found in the little things — being there when he says he will be, offering unsolicited help, remembering the small details that bring joy to you. Consider how lucky you may be to have a man who is true to his word, surprises you with a smile, and goes out of his way to show you how much you mean to him. Some people say things and make promises they have no intention of keeping. Your husband can tell you he loves you as many times as you want, but until his behavior coincides with that, you may not believe his words. Some feelings cannot be expressed merely; they require actions to speak for them. Words are cheap; anyone can tell someone they love them, but they will only feel the immensity of these emotions once they are acted upon. This concept applies to almost every situation in your life. In your marriage, if your husband consistently comes home late from work and does not answer his phone, you may think he is cheating. This is a valid concern since your husband's actions contradict how you desire him to behave. Your suspicion will only grow as the actions contradict the faithful promises that were once made. No protests of love will be able to convince otherwise because actions are looked at over words.

Love is sustained by action. Promises mean nothing without action. You can only learn about your husband's real character by watching his behavior toward you and others. Actions should meet verbal commitments, not conflict with them. If he promises something, you might only believe once he does it. If we give off two contradictory messages, verbal and nonverbal, people will assume the nonverbal over the verbal. We must consistently monitor our actions so that they coincide with the words we say. Words are easy to throw around, but it takes a real man to follow through with actions that back them up.

Your husband may have trouble expressing his emotions verbally because of the way his parents interacted with each other. If children don't see their parents embracing each other and acting lovingly toward one another, they grow up thinking their parents' interaction is unhealthy. Furthermore, if children are not embraced or hugged by their parents as they grow up, they tend to be non-huggers. Actions speak more powerfully than words.

Your husband can repeatedly apologize for his mistakes, but if his actions do not change, the words become meaningless. At the end of the day, whatever your husband's actions may be will show what he is trying to prove. Nothing is happening if he is merely talking, but when actions take place, he is actually engaging in this behavior. Actions prove who someone is, while words only show what someone wants to be.

Whether you have been married for many years or are still getting to know your husband, men are frequently surprised by how often you need to hear "I love you." Although he most certainly does love you, he probably doesn't say these words as usually as you would like to hear. He probably does not fully understand how much it means to you when you hear those words. He may wonder why you need constant reminders of his love because he doesn't need to listen to it repeatedly. Nonetheless, he desperately wants to please you, but he must understand why he is saying "I love you" rather than showing you that he is so important to you.

In today's world, you know women who have had happy marriages and are now divorcing. You also hear about husbands leaving their families over what seems like no good reason at all. Being married can be an enjoyable experience; however, it can leave you feeling vulnerable if you don't hear your husband reassure you that he loves you. While this is very important to you, he believes that you know he loves you by everything he tries to do for you and his children. By telling you how special you are to him, he is reassuring you that your love has not changed; however, he believes you already know that because of what he is doing. With so many stories of partners going astray these days, you often want him to provide the reassurance you need to know that you are the only woman in his life. More than likely, this concept had never occurred to him.

He will probably get it once it is brought to his attention, but this may be an excellent time to let him know how important it is for you to hear those words. Confirm that he is undoubtedly showing you love, but how important it is for you to listen to it said. Many women struggle with insecurities regarding their perceived flaws. He may believe you are perfect, but sometimes you don't see this in yourself. When he tells you he loves you, your confidence rises, and you are again reminded that someone finds you worthy of adoration. It merely means that you value his opinion and enjoy knowing he admires your beautiful qualities. This doesn't mean you are weak; it is just another example of how

God created man and woman. To be clear, he told your husband that he would have to learn to love you.

In a great marriage, both husbands and wives often do many little things that may go unnoticed by their spouse. While you do so many things for him, such as cooking special treats or planning an exciting date, without expecting much in return, you sincerely desire not to be taken for granted either. A simple "I love you" is the perfect way for him to make you feel appreciated. Hearing these words after you have made a special effort translates to more than just a simple thank you.

Finally, remember that living those three little words can be just as crucial as saying them, especially to him. He hopes you will indeed feel loved by demonstrating his love each day in some small way.

About The Author

Dr. Pettigrew received his undergraduate degree at the University of Tennessee, his Master's degree at Murray State University, and his Doctoral degree from the University of Memphis.

Joe has been a high school teacher, university professor, College Dean, and and the CEO for Leaderpoint Consulting Group. He has consulted with many of the most successful corporate leaders in the world and has close ties with many national Christian sports celebrities.

In 2008 he founded the national men's ministry, *In The Zone.* The ministry held in large arenas and churche was closed during Covid-19.

Joe has authored four books. and is currently the Pastor at Brownsville Presbyterian Church in Tennessee.

He has been married to Trudy for over 50 years, and together they have three children: Ashley, Tara, and Tyler. He also has seven grandchildren.

Thanks for reading Cracking The Man Code.

For information about Joe speaking in your church or about ordering additional books, please contact info@inthezone.org.

May God Bless You.